he has connected me to as a mentor. What a responsibility and high privilege to be engaged together in this life-changing process!"

KENNETH A. EPP, Ph.D., Spring Mountain Bible Church,
Portland, Oregon


"Outstanding! Ron Jenson and Ted Engstrom do a masterful job in combining biblical truths and timeless wisdom with practical application. Their use of biblical role models, classic analogies and real-life stories really help to articulate the value of being a godly and effective mentor. Ron and Ted's hearts really came through in their book. They give us insight to what a truly wonderful mentoring relationship looks like. I would recommend this to any person seeking fullness in their life."

DALE VERMILLION, president and CEO of
Vermillion Consulting, Inc.


"For many years the word 'mentoring' scared me to death because of the mental picture I had painted in my mind. However, what I've learned is that mentoring and accountability have brought about a newfound freedom. As a minister, I recognize the landmines and slippery slopes of temptation of trying to go it alone. With the help of God and others, I've been a changed man publicly and privately."

ROD HANDLEY, founder and president of
Character That Counts


A true servant of Christ mentors select people around them. We urgently need a movement of servants who develop leaders the Jesus way— through intentional mentoring. Ron Jensen and Ted Engstrom bring us face to face with the vision, character and heart to make this a reality in our lives and ministries.

DR. STACY T. RINEHART, international director of
MentorLink International

# The making of a
# MENTOR

9 ESSENTIAL CHARACTERISTICS OF INFLUENTIAL CHRISTIAN LEADERS

# The making of a
# MENTOR

9 ESSENTIAL CHARACTERISTICS OF INFLUENTIAL CHRISTIAN LEADERS

## DR. TED W. ENGSTROM
## DR. RON JENSON

**Authentic**

Published in partnership with World Vision Press

Authentic Media
We welcome your comments and questions.
129 Mobilization Drive, Waynesboro, GA 30830 USA authentic@stl.org
and 9 Holdom Avenue, Bletchley, Milton Keynes, Bucks, MK1 1QR, UK
www.authenticbooks.com

If you would like a copy of our current catalog, contact us at:
1-8MORE-BOOKS
ordersusa@stl.org

The Making of a Mentor
ISBN: 1932805-30-3

10 09 08 07 06 05 / 7 6 5 4 3 2 1

Published in 2005 by Authentic Media

Published in partnership with World Vision
34834 Weyerhauser Way South
P.O. Box 9716
Federal Way, WA 98063 USA
www.worldvision.org

Cover design: Grey Matter Group
Interior design: Angela Duerksen
Editorial team: Karen James and Megan Kassebaum

Printed in the United States of America

To those who mentored us,
to the individuals whom
we have had the privilege to mentor,
and especially to our wives.
We thank God for them!

# CONTENTS

# ACKNOWLEDGMENTS

Our deep thanks to all of those who have invested in our lives and allowed us to speak into their lives. We praise God for you!

Our heartfelt thanks to the many, many individuals who shared their stories and insights on mentoring with us. We only wish we could have included everything you told us. This book wouldn't have been possible without your contributions.

Our special thanks to Ron's wife, Mary, who helped us craft and shape the first draft of this book, and to David Sanford, Elizabeth Honeycutt, and the rest of the editorial services team at Sanford Communications, Inc., who helped us revise, enhance, and finish this project.

Our sincere thanks to Tim Beals at World Vision Press, who believed in this book and provided the leadership to make it a reality.

# PREFACE

A s the authors' wives, we couldn't let this book enter the public's hands without some observations. Between us, we've been married nearly 100 years—long enough to have observed our husbands in all sorts of situations with all sorts of individuals.

Neither one of us was surprised that our husbands teamed up to write this book. Nor were we surprised at the men they chose to highlight as their most significant mentors and influencers. The men who marked their lives were and are special friends of ours as well, and we are endlessly grateful for the influence they have had on our husbands' lives, their career paths, and their walks with God—and consequently on ours.

We've not had official mentor/mentoree relationships with our husbands, but we can each testify to the enormous impact their attention has had on us. The principles you will read about in this book apply to good marriages in many instances as well and, though we know we had a part to play in their character, we agree that in our husbands we've been given the greater gift.

We've watched our husbands rise time and again to difficult occasions; we've measured their character; we've observed their behavior. Such scrutiny happens in a marriage. They are not perfect, as we're sure you know. But they are consistent in their attempts to live rightly; they rank high in integrity; they are the same behind closed doors and in public.

It pleases us to see Ted and Ron handing off what they've learned, and continue to learn, to others. We applaud their commitment to being and making mentors!

—*Dorothy Engstrom (1915–2005) and Mary Jenson*

*"You cannot not set an example."*
−MAL KING


*"And the things you have heard me say in the
presence of many witnesses entrust to reliable men
who will also be qualified to teach others."*
−2 TIMOTHY 2:2


*"In this world of ours, that which matters most is not
what happens to the outside of things, but what happens
to the inside of people."*
−WALTER BOWIE

# INTRODUCTION

J esus ministered to many, but he *focused on a few*. Paul, Timothy, and Silas ministered to many but they, too, focused on a few. What makes this strategy so compelling? Why did Jesus and his disciples narrow their attention to small groups of people?

Because they understood the secret of living forward—spiritual multiplication through intentionally influencing a few people at a time. They knew that by concentrating on a few faithful men and women they would leave behind them a legacy of people whose influence would extend beyond a generation or two; in fact, a legacy that would continue to multiply until the return of the Lord.

This book is written to stimulate you—whatever your age, gender, or position in life—toward a passionate desire to change people who will then change other people who will change other people. You will see men and women who influenced others in a significant way both by formal and informal mentoring. The key is not so much *how* you pour your life into people but *that you are a person worth following*. God placed you here to give your life away as you live and speak truth into the lives of others.

> God placed you here to
> **give your life**
> **away** as you live and
> speak truth into the
> lives of others.

## THE CALL TO MENTOR

As you study the Scripture, you'll discover the healthiest church in the New Testament—the church at Thessalonica. These are the believers that Paul praised for their "work produced by faith, your labor prompted by love, and your endurance inspired by hope in our Lord Jesus Christ."

This church manifested a dynamic, faith-filled, and powerful lifestyle because of the leadership of those who built the church initially. Three men, Paul, Timothy, and Silas, moved into the city and spent concentrated time pouring their lives into the Thessalonian church. These distinctly different men demonstrated nine core leadership traits—traits that we believe can transform lives today as they did two thousand years ago. These traits are encouragement, self-discipline, gentleness, affection, strong communication, honesty, servanthood, godliness, and the willingness to confront.

Paul described their mentoring plan in 1 Thessalonians 2:7-12:

> But we were gentle among you, like a mother caring for her little children. We loved you so much that we were delighted to share with you not only the gospel of God but our lives as well, because you had become so dear to us. Surely you remember, brothers, our toil and hardship; we worked night and day in order not to be a burden to anyone while we preached the gospel of God to you. You are witnesses, and so is God, of how holy, righteous and blameless

we were among you who believed. For you know that we dealt with each of you as a father deals with his own children, encouraging, comforting and urging you to live lives worthy of God, who calls you into his kingdom and glory.

The Bible illustrates the need for relationships. David and Jonathan had a committed friendship. Moses shared a close relationship with Aaron. Naomi counseled Ruth. Jesus developed deep friendships with the apostles (particularly Peter, James, and John). Paul was close to the elders of the churches he helped to found.

Scripture is clear in stating that we need other people; we need relationships. Psychologists also recognize this need. Harry Stack Sullivan, an eminent psychiatrist in the field of interpersonal relationships, has put forth the theory that "all personal damage and regression, as well as all personal healing and growth, come through our relationships with others. There is a persistent, if uninformed, suspicion in most of us that we can solve our own problems and be the masters of our ships of life. But the fact of the matter is that by ourselves we can only be consumed by our problems and suffer shipwreck."

"By ourselves we can only be consumed by our problems and suffer shipwreck."

OUR STORY

We would like to share our story of mentoring to demonstrate the power of multiplication in mentoring. Ted Engstrom mentored Ron Jenson who mentored his son, Matt Jenson. Matt mentored Mark Bilby. Here's the story:

*Ted and Ron*—Ted is one of the leading Christian statesmen of the past century. His name is often connected with Bill Bright, Billy Graham, and others of that level. He has directly and indirectly touched the lives of millions of people. But just let me (Ron) give you a glimpse of his breadth of influence.

Before I ever met Ted, he had been mentoring me for years through his books on leadership and management. When I sat through a seminar he gave on leadership, I was struck by his grace, wisdom, practicality, and eagerness to learn. That day he became one of my heroes—a role he has kept for over twenty-five years. When I became the president of Campus Crusade's International School of Theology, I turned to Ted as a friend and mentor.

He not only gave me great counsel, but he constantly modeled servant leadership, was concerned for me and my family, and championed me to my team and to his own friends and colleagues. Ted often drops me a note or gives me a call just to say that he's proud of me and to encourage me. His hard work, uncanny wisdom, and his experience are paying big dividends in my life today.

*Ron and Matt*—Matt has this to say about his mentoring relationship with his dad, "When people ask me what I've learned from my dad, I think of grace. I can't think of a time when I wasn't able to bring all of life—pretty ugly as much of it is—before my dad for his counsel, teaching, conviction, and overwhelming love. Once I confessed a particularly discouraging sin to him. Ashamed and deflated, I felt wind return to my sails as he said, 'Boy, been there, done that! Isn't that frustrating?'

"My dad was intentional when he asked me (as a six-year-old) to join him for weekly breakfasts with a quiver of highlighters and the book of Proverbs. He was teaching me to love the Word, to be shaped by it. He was teaching me straight-line living before I had carved curved ruts too deep to easily drive out of.

"Dad's been relationally intentional. This has included programs (the Proverbs breakfasts, the sex-talk disguised as a fishing trip, and including me in on a trip to Asia which exposed me to poverty, different cultures, and big things of God). It's included lots of time and space together. It's included teachable moments. Those are what I remember most vividly.

"He knows about almost everything going on in my life, and consequently he has permission to speak into anything going on in my life. I figured his influence would wane with my maturity, but if anything, I'm hungrier for it more than ever.

"Before my senior year of high school, my dad took me to a Promise Keeper's pastors' conference. One thing that came out of that conference was the beginning of a small prayer and accountability group. I met with a brand-new believer and two Catholics, and we talked very frankly about areas where we needed serious work and we prayed for one another.

"The new believer was Mark Bilby. We spent a lot of time together, and he gained his spiritual sea legs that year. Recently, I stood by his side as he married Tamara, and I marveled at the good work of our God. Mark is a pastor, studying for his doctorate in historical theology. We're reciprocal disciplers these days—what the Bible calls 'iron sharpening iron,' 'bearing one another's burdens,' and 'speaking the truth in love.'"

*Matt and Mark*—Mark Bilby's story continues the mentoring multiplication. He says, "When we were in high school, Matt invited me to play basketball with him on a regular basis. His friendship came at just the right time in my life, when I was becoming disillusioned with other so-called friends.

"Without seeming to force things, Matt would bring up Jesus while we were having a good time. It was easy to see and hear that he thought Jesus was the greatest person anyone could ever know. The Lord was as real and living to him as any other friend.

"Matt met me where I was in the faith. Previous offers to know Jesus had seemed forced or contrived, but Matt's approach was entirely new. Matt's life was as much of a testimony as his words were. Something that I saw then and still see today is the exemplary character that Matt displays. He is almost dogged in his consistency, in terms of keeping his word, being committed to friends, and patiently urging the Lord's best for others, whether they are Christians or not.

"A few years ago, I had the opportunity to lead a person back to Christ who had grown up in the faith and had become disillusioned with the church. I was able to help him walk through the Bible and think through some tough issues. We began meeting for accountability and prayer on a regular basis, and this group eventually grew to include a few other people. This person saw Jesus in me, found a friend in me, and rediscovered Jesus as his Shepherd."

Ted mentored Ron. Ron mentored Matt. Matt mentored Mark. Now Mark is a pastor and is mentoring others. Although both of us (Ted and Ron) have mentored numerous individuals, we include these stories to show the lasting effect of a godly mentor.

The **potential is incredible** for your mentoring relationship to be **multiplied many times over.**

Second Timothy 2:2 says, "And the things you have heard me say in the presence of many witnesses entrust to reliable men who will also be qualified to teach others." In this way, the mentoring process can live on long after you have gone to be with the Lord. Godly mentoring will be multiplied as your protégés pass on to others what they have learned from you. In the same way, your mentoree's mentorees will pass on their skills and knowledge. The potential is incredible for your mentoring relationship to be multiplied many times over.

WHAT IS MENTORING?

For the Christian, mentoring has objectives in the real world that go beyond success and advancement, to personal significance and healthy relationships with God and others. Mentoring can be done on the corporate level as well as on the ministry level. Mentoring does not focus solely on the spiritual, but incorporates everything that is of value to the mentor and mentoree.

A mentor provides modeling, close supervision on special projects, and individualized help in many areas—discipline, encouragement, correction, confrontation, and a calling to accountability. While the focus of mentoring involves the Christian development of the mentoree, it is not limited to that. Mentoring is a broad term describing the process of assisting a man or woman to develop his or her maximum potential in Jesus Christ regardless of vocation.

Some mentoring is not done deliberately. This could be true in the corporate world, where a leader inspires growth and advancement without intentionally investing time in his colleagues. It could be true of a pastor whose stellar example promotes holiness and a passion for people. This is often true of parent and child relationships. However, the most effective mentoring is usually deliberate and intentional.

"Mentoring is **giving encouragement** to those who rely on your **wisdom** and the **knowledge** you have gathered during your lifetime."

Ted's daughter, JoAnn Bengel, describes mentoring this way, "Mentoring is giving encouragement to those who rely on your wisdom and the knowledge you have gathered during your lifetime."

Mentoring can be done between individuals of the same age or those whose ages span many generations. Women and men both make great mentors. Generally, it is best for women to mentor women and men to mentor men but there are exceptions to this.

## THE IMPORTANCE OF MENTORING

To the Christian believer, there is no greater "mentor" than the Lord Jesus Christ. How he fashioned his meek-spirited followers into an invincible company of over-comers is a display of divine mentoring to which we can only aspire. Unlike Christ, we cannot bring about change in other people's lives. As God, he has the power to soften hearts and change lives. We are not the Holy Spirit but we *are* called to inspire, promote, and facilitate whole, authentic living.

The Christian mentor takes his example from Christ's life and work. The same qualities that characterized his perfect life can also mark our own. We will be most like Christ—and most effective as mentors—when we develop the following nine traits: encouragement, self-discipline, gentleness, affection, strong communication, honesty, servanthood, godliness, and the willingness to confront.

If you desire those things, you've come to the right place. How do you become a mentor? The place to start is found in these nine attributes. Read along as we discover together the qualities that make an excellent mentor who has the ability to change generations of lives for eternity.

*"Our chief want in life is somebody who shall make us do what we can."*
—RALPH WALDO EMERSON

*"You have it easily in your power to increase the sum total of this world's happiness now. How? By giving a few words of sincere appreciation to someone who is lonely or discouraged. Perhaps you will forget tomorrow the kind words you say today, but the recipient may cherish them over a lifetime."*
—DALE CARNEGIE

# Chapter 1

# ENCOURAGEMENT

**W**hat kind of mentor impacts the whole world? It is a person of *vision* who has the ability to see potential in his protégé, a person who is not intimidated by difficulties. Mentors have the ability to see positive change in their mentoree, especially if they are actively involved in encouraging the mentoree's growth and development. A positive word, a motivating nudge, an expression of belief in your protégé will make all the difference in the mentoring process.

### BELIEVE IN YOUR MENTOREE
*Believe in a mentoree's potential.* Bobb Biehl says, "You have to look at the protégé and say, 'Yes, I think this person has tremendous potential. I think if I invest some of my life in him, he has what it takes to be all that he can be.'"

*Dream of the mentoree's future.* Again, Bobb Biehl says, "Look into the eyes of your mentoree and see what he feels in his heart but has never thought yet in his head. He might feel like he has tremendous potential but won't allow himself to think that yet. He places limits on himself that the mentor has to eliminate. Help your protégé to see what you feel is his potential, even though he might not yet see it. Put that into words, don't just think it. Tell him, 'You have the potential. Go for it!'"

This can be seen in my (Ron) own life. I was rescued as a thirteen-year-old by a man named Don Anderson. When I was a little kid, I was a troublemaker. I almost flunked kindergarten. The teacher said that I was "socially maladjusted" which really meant that I got in fights all the time. I fought because I had a poor self-concept. I weighed 140 pounds when I was ten years old (and I wasn't very tall!). My nickname was "Jelly Belly Jenson."

**Believe** in your mentoree's potential and abilities. **Dream** of your mentoree's future.

I was getting in trouble at home and at school, taking home solid D's. My fourth grade report card had a D average in grades but straight "excellents" in effort. What does that say to a kid? "Ronnie is really stupid but he is maximizing his potential." That's how I saw my life—dumb and maximizing myself.

Then, when I was thirteen, a friend invited me to a church camp where I heard the gospel for the first time. I gave my life to Christ, and a change began. But I had many bad habits that could have threatened my spiritual growth.

The difference was Don Anderson. He met with me, and several others, on a weekly basis for about three months. He taught us basic follow up material, but what I most vividly remember is that he searched each week to find something in my life that he could praise. And he had to work pretty hard; I didn't have a lot to work with.

One week he said, "Ronnie, you talk a lot. Now, what you have to say isn't that good, but you have some verbal skills. One day you might become a speaker." He also said, "Ronnie, kids follow you. Now, son, you're not always going the right direction, but you have some leadership skills, and one day you could become a leader." Every week he did this for me.

Within months my life began to change. I went from fighting to becoming the student body president of our junior high school. I lost a lot of weight and began to play and excel in multiple sports. My grades went from D's to A's and stayed there throughout my education.

Was I smarter? No. Was I a more gifted leader? Not really. Was I a great athlete? Nope. I was motivated! All because Don Anderson forever touched my life by mentoring me through *belief* and *encouragement* for a few short months.

Another man who influenced my life in a profound way is Bill Bright. When I was young, Bill believed in me. I was way too young and inexperienced to run a graduate school, but Bill believed in me enough to allow me to fill that role. When things got tough during my tenure, I was always amazed at how he listened, loved, and moved people toward unity of spirit.

Bill believed in me and gave me permission to believe in myself. His constant words of encouragement, honest affection, and consistent faith not only bolstered me but made me a man whom God could use. That impact poured over to my wife and my children.

## WORDS OF ENCOURAGEMENT

Mentoring through affirmation—the idea may not be revolutionary but the impact of your positive words can be. Search for character traits (such as vulnerability or commitment), areas of improvement (e.g. "I've noticed that you have made improvements in controlling your temper"), or ways that they are making great effort ("Thank you for taking the time to read the book I suggested last week"). When your protégé knows that you are noticing, and appreciating his good choices and efforts, he will be encouraged to continue on. There is nothing as discouraging as putting a large amount of effort into pleasing someone who doesn't notice what you've done.

Don't discourage your mentoree by your silence. Though you may feel positive about your protégé, it is in vain if he never knows. Vocalize your encouragement, but be sure that you are genuine. Search for qualities or special efforts that are commendable and then share heartfelt encouragement. It has been said that "we wildly underestimate the power of the tiniest personal touch of kindness."

> "We wildly underestimate the **power** of the tiniest **personal touch** of kindness."

If you feel the need to share healthy criticism, refer to chapter 9 for suggestions. Remember, "A gentle answer turns away wrath, but a harsh word stirs up anger. . . . The tongue that brings healing is a tree of life, but a deceitful tongue crushes the spirit" (Proverbs 15:1, 4).

Coaching by affirmation—and the genius of Harry Hopman—built an Australian dynasty in world tennis. He coached a slow-footed boy whom he nicknamed "Rocket;" he had a weak, frail boy whom he named "Muscles." They became "Rocket" Rod Laver and Ken "Muscles" Rosewall, champions of world tennis because of affirmation.

Jesus did the same thing. Remember the disciple who was impetuous, rash, and always putting his foot in his mouth? Jesus called him just the opposite. Petros: Peter, the Rock. Jesus didn't call him what he was, but what he would become.

You can encourage people by complimenting them. This is not flattery; flattery is praising people for qualities over which they have no control. Flattery highlights physical characteristics such as clothing or belongings. Praise and compliments are used properly when they are given for qualities that people are developing in their lives. For example, you can praise your protégé for her increasing love for others, seen in her growing selfless service.

Jesus praised his men for faith. Paul repeatedly praised his coworkers and believers in the early church for positive qualities in their lives, such as love and hope.

Everyone desires this type of compliment. William James said, "The deepest principle of human nature is the craving to be appreciated." Spoken or written compliments carry an almost unimaginable weight. When they become habits, the people around you flourish.

## EXPRESSING CONFIDENCE

We need to show our mentorees that we have confidence in them not only when they are doing well but also when they make mistakes.

Jesus poured his life into the twelve disciples. He was crucified and went through the very painful burden of the crucifixion compounded with suffering the humiliation of God. After the resurrection, he visited the eleven disciples in the upper room.

The average person would have delivered a different message than Jesus did at that time. After all, the disciples had lived with Jesus for three years of intense ministry. In front of their eyes, he raised the dead, healed the sick, and fed the multitudes. He had told them that he would die and rise again. Yet all of them ran away and hid when he was taken away to be killed. Peter even denied Jesus three times.

Jesus had every right to respond negatively to the lack of faith shown by his disciples. Instead, he told them, "All authority in heaven and on earth has been given to me. Therefore go and make disciples of all nations . . . " (Matthew 28:18–20). Jesus placed the authority and responsibility for the spiritual outcome of the world and the generations to come on these men— these "failures." Rather than reprimanding them for their failure, or giving up on them, Jesus placed the future of his Church in their hands.

Jesus knew how to believe in men. He didn't rub their faces in the ground when they failed, but he told them that he believed in them. He expressed confidence in them.

Howard Hendricks, the great Bible teacher, tells the story of when he was in the fifth grade. He was such a bad boy that the teacher used to tie his hands and feet to a chair and gag him.

On the first day of sixth grade, as he walked in and saw his new teacher, he heard, "So you are Howie Hendricks! I've heard a lot about you!" Hendricks thought, "Oh no, I'm dead!" Then the teacher knelt down beside him, looked him in the eye and said, "And I don't believe a word of it." The teacher believed in him. The result paid off: Howie Hendricks was a sweet boy throughout the rest of school.

*Verbalize your belief in the individuals you mentor.*

Most people have never reached even half of their potential because no one has believed in them. You can be a man or woman of great impact by verbalizing your belief in the people you mentor. If they have failed, sweep the past behind them, don't let them be paralyzed by their past failures. Keep telling them that you believe they will be used for great things and that they are people of great worth. Keep on verbalizing it until it becomes a part of their life.

## COMFORT

Encouraging implies supporting, sustaining, and comforting other people. One of the roles of a mentor is to comfort people in their times of need. 2 Corinthians 1:3–4 says, "Praise be to the God and Father of our Lord Jesus Christ, the Father of compassion and the God of all comfort, who comforts us in all our troubles, so that we can comfort those in any trouble with the comfort we ourselves have received from God." In other words, if you have received any comfort from God, then you are to give comfort to anyone with any trouble. But don't just give your own comfort; we are to comfort with the comfort we have received from God.

Paul says that our job is to learn to encourage by comforting others in the same way that we have received comfort from God. One of the reasons that God allows us to go through great difficulties is so that we might be able to empathize, understand, and help others in trouble. 2 Corinthians 7:5-7 illustrates this, "For when we came into Macedonia, this body of ours had no rest, but we were harassed at every turn—conflicts on the outside, fears within. But God, who comforts the downcast, comforted us by the coming of Titus, and not only by his coming but also by the comfort you had given him. He told us about your longing for me, your deep sorrow, your ardent concern for me, so that my joy was greater than ever."

God uses men and women to comfort other people. An effective mentor can put himself in his mentoree's shoes. He has the capacity to feel deeply with people, to empathize, and to tell people through his life how much he loves and cares for them.

First Thessalonians 3:1-7 says:

> So when we could stand it no longer, we thought it best to be left by ourselves in Athens. We sent Timothy, who is our brother and God's fellow worker in spread-

ing the gospel of Christ, to strengthen and encourage you in your faith, so that no one would be unsettled by these trials. . . . Timothy has just now come to us from you and has brought good news about your faith and love. He has told us that you always have pleasant memories of us and that you long to see us, just as we also long to see you. Therefore, brothers, in all our distress and persecution we were encouraged about you because of your faith.

**Words of encouragement can literally lift our protégé's burden of trials and hardships.**

Timothy brought encouraging news to Paul and Silas about the Thessalonian church. His positive words about the Thessalonians brought a relief from their distress and persecution. Timothy's encouragement to the Thessalonian believers and his encouraging report to Paul and Silas brought joy and satisfaction to everyone involved. Our lives should be no different; our words of encouragement can literally lift our protégé's burden of trials and hardships.

BECOMING SONS AND DAUGHTERS OF ENCOURAGEMENT

Barnabas was a disciple and apostle in the early Church. His name was originally Joseph, but the apostles renamed him Barnabas, meaning Son of Encouragement. That's what he was to the apostles (Acts 4:36). Paul and Barnabas traveled together, prayed together, and shared in ministry all across Asia Minor. We have record of their journeys in the early chapters of the book of Acts.

When the gospel first went to the Gentiles, Barnabas was sent to Antioch to investigate. Many people had believed the message about Jesus. "When he (Barnabas) arrived and saw the evidence of the grace of God, he was glad and encouraged them all to remain true to the Lord with all their hearts. He was a good man, full of the Holy Spirit and faith" (Acts 11:23–24). His life was so characterized by encouragement that the apostles renamed him "son of encouragement"!

What would people "rename" you? Would encouragement come to their minds? Take a moment to think about the way that you use your words (or lack of words). Do people smile with satisfaction and joy as they leave the conversation with you? Or do they feel a cloud of worry and sarcasm?

The Barnabas in my (Ted) life was a gentleman named Dr. F. Carleton Booth. I first came to know Carleton when I joined the staff at World Vision in California, and he was serving as secretary/treasurer of our board of directors, as well as the professor of evangelism at Fuller Theological Seminary. Carleton had an office near mine at the World Vision headquarters, and several times in the course of a week he would come to the office to spend a few minutes handling mail and consulting with staff members as an unofficial chaplain.

Invariably as I had challenges and important decisions to make in my leadership role, I would go to Carleton's office to ask for his prayer support and godly wisdom. In our consulting, he would always hold in confidence what we shared together but was available to give wise direction and counsel. We always closed our conversation by a time of prayer together. His mentoring to me was invaluable and unforgettable.

In addition, we shared in a host of public meetings, Bible conferences, camps, and evangelistic services. I would have the privilege of bringing the message and he would, in his inimitable way, lead the congregational singing. He was a master chorister and deeply loved by all those who attended these gatherings.

Sometimes I was a bit impulsive in reprimanding people who reported to me. Often Carleton would urge caution and suggest that I take my time before facing that individual with guidance and words of correction. His cautions to me were always much appreciated and most helpful.

I learned so very much, simply by being with him, listening to him, and seeking his wisdom. Every leader needs to have a Barnabas in his life. I am so grateful for my Barnabas, Carleton Booth.

As Christian mentors, our responsibility is to bring comfort, exhortation, and encouragement to those who look to us for guidance. Your words have the power of "life" and "death," of success and failure, of growth and stagnation. Choose words that will encourage your mentoree to become the man or woman that God designed them to be. Motivate them to pursue God's best in every area of their life by your encouraging words of life.

Choose **words** that will **encourage** your mentoree to become the woman or man that **God designed** them to be.

*"Encouragement must be not only by words but also by deeds. The mentoree needs encouragement in opportunities. In the past few years, I have said to some young evangelists, 'Come with me.' This has meant that I have stepped aside and let them preach. This can be risky; especially in cross-cultural situations. In the case of two young men who accompanied me to Africa, I came away with great admiration. When they invited people to respond, many came forward. God blesses only what we risk for him.*

*"There is also the need for regular encouragement in finances. We are called to live 'by faith' but not 'on faith.' And if faith is to grow it must be recompensed, in due season.*

*"I thank God for the few encouragers who came my way in the early years of my training and ministry and for the financial sacrifices they made. Some of these people are now in glory, but I still remember when I was with OC International, two sisters who died of cancer. One of their last deeds on earth was to contribute to my ministry. There was Pastor George Robinson in Jamestown, North Dakota, where I went to college, who got me invited to some little country churches in the area. I think of my college language professor, Mr. Arthur Ellingson, who asked me to write a term paper on the French Revolution in French and Spanish. When I finished it he said, 'Mr. Thomas, this is not as good as I hoped it would be. But knowing the conditions under which you wrote it, I am giving you a "B."' At that time, I was working in a hotel six nights a week*

*from 11 p.m. to 7 a.m. Today, I do my own preaching in French and Spanish."*

—DR. BILL THOMAS (Th.D. Free University of Amsterdam) is an international American who lives in Strasbourg, France. He is president of the Bill Thomas Evangelist Association and is a partner evangelist with the Luis Palau Evangelistic Association's Next Generation Alliance.

*"I've found that all of us need an encouraging word, and when that word comes from our mentor, it can be especially powerful and meaningful. On more than one occasion I have been called by men who I have been in a formal mentoring relationship with. When they call for no other reason other than to just say, 'I was just thinking about you, and I'm grateful to God for you,' then their words have always been soaked up by my soul. I've saved letters from my mentors that came at a time when I needed to know someone other than my wife believed in me. I have a collection of e-mails that I never deleted. Why? Because God has always used words to bring hope, courage, and strength. And we all need them from time to time."*

—DR. DENNIS RAINEY is the president and the cofounder of FamilyLife. He and his wife, Barbara, have been married for thirty-two years, are the parents of six children, and recently welcomed their seventh grandchild. They live near Little Rock, Arkansas.

*"I admire people who always know what to say, when to say it, and where. These are folks who encourage with thoughtful words straight from the heart. I met two such people after I got out of the hospital in 1968. I was facing*

*a life of total paralysis with no idea of what to do or who to turn to for help. Thankfully, God brought two friends into my life who mentored me through that tumultuous time of fear and anxiety—they envisioned success for me when I was too weak and too frightened to envision it for myself. And a month later? I was well on my way to the future, signing up for my church choir and classes at the University of Maryland. I say 'Amen!' to the counsel and advice shared in this powerful chapter. My only question is: how did those friends read the draft back in 1968?"*

—JONI EARECKSON TADA is founder and CEO of Joni and Friends, an international organization which accelerates Christian ministry in the disability community worldwide. A quadriplegic, Joni works as a tireless advocate for disabled persons from her wheelchair, as she has for thirty-eight years. She and her husband Ken reside in Calabasas, California. If you are mentoring a family affected by disability, contact www.joniandfriends.org for information and resources.

*"'Flatter me, and I may not believe you. Criticize me, and I may not like you. Ignore me, and I may not forgive you. Encourage me, and I will not forget you.'*

*"No, we do not forget those who have encouraged us along the way. Encouragement can be general like saying a kind word, or quite specific with a goal in mind. I am forever grateful for the encouragement that Luis Palau has given through the years in very specific ways.*

*"He first gave me some general encouragement with the words that I would one day preach to the masses around the world. That in itself was a gift that I needed, since*

*many people were criticizing me for wanting to be an evangelist. But then Luis went beyond the general kind and began to give me specific encouragement.*

*"First he asked me at the young age of thirty if I would like to join his organization. He helped pay for my way to Amsterdam 86 (a crusade) so that I could meet and hear other evangelists. He allowed me the opportunity to preach along side him at various events around the world. He not only encouraged me with words, but with opportunities!*

*"The most specific encouragement I received from Luis came after he listened to me preach one night. As we talked later in the evening he said, 'Dan, take your time, you are rushing your invitation. People need time to think and to do business with the Lord. Don't rush it; give them more time before you close the invitation.' I have never forgotten those words. Every time I give an invitation in the U.S. or overseas I still remember the words of Luis Palau and extend the invitation a little longer. There will be folks in heaven that will thank Luis for giving me that encouragement!"*

—DAN OWENS is a popular author, conference speaker, evangelist and evangelism trainer. He serves as president of Eternity Minded Ministries in San Diego, California.

*"I think that this chapter is right on the mark. Everyone responds to encouragement especially if it is sincere. On the tennis court I have found that if you can frame some instruction around two pieces of positive or encouraging advice then the student will really be receptive and try what you are suggesting. If he hears only criticism or*

*negative feedback with no encouragement, then he will get discouraged or even give up.*

*"Everyone has abilities and qualities to praise, so it really doesn't take too much to find a way to encourage someone and give her something of which to proud. I have been amazed at the way people can respond with just a little bit of encouragement whether they are young or old. So many people get so little feedback of this type that they relish any bit of encouragement that they get, and it can even be a life changing moment.*

*"Once you have encouraged someone you can later exhort him to follow a dream that could lead him to something special. If nothing else, you can put a smile on an uncertain face that could light up the day."*

—STAN SMITH is a Wimbledon and U.S. Open champion with thirty-nine career singles titles and sixty-one career doubles titles. He served as the director of coaching for the United States Tennis Association from 1988 to 1993. He was the coach of the men's Olympic tennis team for the 2000 games in Sydney. In 2002, Stan co-founded the Smith-Stearns Tennis Academy at Sea Pines Resort.

## HOW ABOUT YOU?

Determine your level of proficiency in the area of encouragement from the chart below. 1 is the lowest, 10 is the highest with 5 as average.

ENCOURAGEMENT

| 1 | 1.5 | 2 | 2.5 | 3 | 3.5 | 4 | 4.5 | 5 | 5.5 | 6 | 6.5 | 7 | 7.5 | 8 | 8.5 | 9 | 9.5 | 10 |
|---|-----|---|-----|---|-----|---|-----|---|-----|---|-----|---|-----|---|-----|---|-----|-----|

What do you need to do in order to improve half of a point this week in your mentoring relationships?

*"My worth to God in public
is what I am in private."*
−OSWALD CHAMBERS

*"Be what you would have your pupils to be."*
−THOMAS CARLYLE

# Chapter 2

# SELF-DISCIPLINE

In 1967, I (Ron) was entering my sophomore year of college and had just been mentored by Bill Bright. He had "taught" me how to do evangelism, and I was feeling pretty good about myself. I went out and witnessed and had led someone to Christ for the first time. I felt so confident.

A couple of weeks later, I went to a parade with a friend. I observed a man walking alongside the parade, handing out tracts. People were laughing and making fun of him. At that time, I thought that the only way to "do evangelism" was to talk to someone and share the Four Spiritual Laws. I thought, "He's doing it all wrong!"

I wanted to tell this man how he should communicate the gospel the right way. I grabbed him by the shoulders and said, "I appreciate that you're sharing the gospel, but if you really love people, you'll talk to them and not just cram a tract at them."

He said "Ala ala ala." He didn't have a tongue. He was sharing the gospel the only way he could. I learned an important lesson that day: to watch my tongue and not jump to conclusions. Ultimately, I needed to learn to have self-control and self-discipline in my interactions with other people.

In the Bible, Paul discusses the need for self-control and self-sacrifice. Keeping your life and mentoring in balance involves disciplining your use of time and resources, keeping free from distractions and sin, and being willing to sacrifice.

## LEADING AN EXEMPLARY LIFE

Proverbs 25:28 says, "Like a city whose walls are broken down is a man who lacks self-control." If you don't have self-control, anything can have mastery over you. Like a city whose protective walls have come down, a man with no self-control is defenseless. Whether it's the temptation to pass along a juicy bit of gossip or the lure of lying to save face—or something even more serious—sin is allowed to creep in when self-control is lacking. A sinful lifestyle without self-control is unfit for mentoring.

The book of Proverbs calls a person with no self-control a fool. A fool cannot hope to make a positive difference in the lives of those around him. Instead, mentors with self-control have learned to set and maintain positive habits in their personal lives.

> If you don't have self-control, anything can have mastery over you.

Bill Kliewer was mentored by Ted and shares the following about Ted's personal habits, "At the heart of everything Ted talks about is the importance of spiritual transformation and a relationship with Jesus Christ. Therefore, at World Vision, our spoken and unspoken goal was first and foremost the transformation of people by moving them toward a relationship with God through Jesus Christ. Ted did it corporately by building it into job expectations, and he did it personally by living out his character in front of us.

"Ted is consistent. You can always count on him. He is appropriately predictable as he follows his basic principles and daily schedule. Meetings are always on time. When he says 9:00 a.m., he means it. Ted taught me the importance of returning messages, mail, and e-mail within a certain time frame. If you discuss something with Ted and follow-up is necessary, there is never any question as to whether it will get done or not. He is totally responsible and consistent at every level. Ted has impressed upon me the importance of honesty. 'White lies' are unacceptable. Now and then, we have discussed what Jesus would do in certain situations."

## KEEPING FREE FROM SIN

Sin has the ability to keep you from being effective in mentoring as well as the other areas of your life. James tells us that "we all stumble in many ways" (3:2). While we live in a fallen state in a fallen world, we won't reach perfection. Only Jesus Christ accomplished perfection as a human. But we cannot tolerate sin in our lives if we hope to be like Christ and have our mentorees also be like Christ. While we cannot reach perfection, we are called to strive for holiness. Sin has no part—no place—in the Christian's life.

> We **cannot** tolerate sin in our lives if we hope to be like Christ.

Even if your mentoring is on the secular level, such as business mentoring, your personal holiness must be a top priority. You can have no say in others' lives when you have no control over your own.

Since mistakes and sins are an unfortunate part of this life, we must find an appropriate way to deal with our errors. Purity in the Christian life is not the absence of sin; instead, it involves the pursuit of holiness in every area of life. When you sin, confess first to the Lord and then confess to those people that your sin has affected. Confession allows us to keep short accounts and to live with a clean conscience. We can experience true forgiveness and restoration when we confess our sins to God. First John 1:9 says, "If we confess our sins, he is faithful and just and will forgive us our sins and purify us from all unrighteousness."

Repentance is similar to confession, but it also implies willingness to change and a conscious turning away from sin. Be sure that when you confess your sins, you also repent. Intentionally turn yourself away from sin and turn *toward righteousness.*

For example, if you find it hard to remain emotionally faithful to your spouse while away on business, you might first determine to stay away from sins that would break that faithfulness. But you must also plan to pursue righteousness by taking whatever measures are necessary. Invite a business partner (of the same gender) to eat dinner with you and room with you. Give your spouse a phone call and set up photos of your family to remind yourself of your resolve. We can never be too strict with ourselves if we are pursuing righteousness and a clean conscience before God. Such deliberate turning toward righteousness will give you a "right" to speak into your protégé's life.

## OVERCOMING OLD HABITS

Kicking an old habit is one of the toughest things to do. It takes hard work and a process of change, but it is an essential element of the disciplined mentor's life. Follow the seven "D's" below in order to beat a bad habit. (Or, you can share this list with your mentoree as needed.)

*Discern the problem*—acknowledge and identify what needs to change in your life. This is the crucial first step; if you do not realize that you have a problem, you have no hope of mending it.

*Discover the biblical alternative*—search the Scriptures for positive examples of good habits you would like to have. If your bad habit is laziness, examine the life of Paul for the alternative (i.e. hard work and perseverance).

*Discard the opportunity to sin*—an addiction to pornography or chat rooms may involve cutting off your internet service. A habit of eating too many sweets may involve throwing out (and committing to not purchase) candy, ice cream, and cookies.

*Disconnect the chain of sin*—anything that ties you to your sin must be broken. Do you friends encourage you to drink too much? Make new friends; or at least restrict your relationship to visits in "safe" locations (such as a coffee shop) and phone conversations. Does your television suck away the prime hours of your day? Give it away. Do your credit cards give you a false sense of wealth that you do not really have? Cancel them. Don't allow yourself to still be connected to the things that cause you to sin.

*Dwell on your whole relationship with Christ*—your relationship with Christ should encompass every area of your life. If you find that you are only coming to him to confess and beg forgiveness, you need to widen your horizons. Commit to praying for your family and friends.

Read the Bible with the conviction that God loves you and desires to reveal himself to you as a loving Father, not just a Judge.

*Drill the new pattern into your life*—habits aren't broken in an instant. New habits can't be formed that quickly, either. It takes persistence and commitment. Do commit to your new patterns and ask a trusted friend to check up on how you're doing.

> You will find victory over sin as you commit to the process of change.

Don't get discouraged if the process of changing your habits is long. Once your new habits are set, you will find it more natural to resist the old strongholds of sin. It may never get "easy," but you will find victory over sin as you commit to the process of change. Robert Ringer said "Success is a matter of understanding and rigorously applying simple habits that always lead to success."

## DISCIPLINE OF RESOURCES

An undisciplined life is often characterized by unwise use of time, money, and other resources. Your date book and checkbook reveal much about the state of your self-control. Identify the resources that God has given you. Then, take some time to examine your self-control and use of these resources. It may be necessary to make changes in order for self-discipline to be a marker of your entire life. Can your mentoree see evidence of your self-controlled life reflected in the choices and behaviors you practice?

For me (Ron), self-discipline involved losing extra weight and becoming physically fit. I realized (through the loving confrontation of a friend) that I could not hope to impact a maximum number of people for the Lord if I allowed my poor health to take years off of my life.

What area of your life lacks self-control? If it involves your time, your money, your health, your training and education, or your gifting, then it involves the resources that God has entrusted to you. Take the time to work through the process of changing negative habits and replacing them with positive self-control (see the "seven D's" above). Once your own life is "controlled," you will be fit for mentoring in these areas.

An **undisciplined** life is often **characterized** by unwise use of **time,** **money,** and other **resources.**

## MENTORED MENTORS

No one is above being mentored, no matter how mature and experienced they are. Consider having a mentor as well as being a mentor. This may help you stay on track—and improve—in areas of your life that are troublesome.

God designed the Christian experience to be best brought out in community. Commit to a local church and get involved. Ask someone you admire to pray for you and meet with you periodically. The things you glean from another life of faithfulness to God will not be wasted.

If you don't have a potential mentor, consider an accountability group. These can range from approximately two to six people and are often comprised of people in the same stage of life. In an accountability group, it is a good idea to just have members of the same sex together.

Resolve to spend concentrated time together in the Word and in prayer for one another. Be open about your struggles and mistakes and allow others to do the same (of course, there must be strict confidentiality).

For many, many years I (Ted) met for breakfast one Friday a month with five other men. We all had different backgrounds, but we were all mature Christians. We all met for a couple of hours each month. It wasn't a Bible study; it wasn't a prayer meeting (although we did pray together). We just shared with each other.

One time I came to the group, very tired because I had been traveling a lot, and said, "Boys, I'm tired, and I'm spiritually down and low." I thought I would get some sympathy out of them, but it didn't happen.

One guy said, "How much time are you spending in the Word these days?"

I said, "Well, not enough as I should I suppose. I've been trying, but I've been busy."

He said, "Yeah, I know that, but answer me, how much time have you been spending in the Word these days?"

I said, "Not as much as I should."

Another guy said, "Then what's your prayer life like?"

I said, "You're butting into my private life now!"

He answered, "I know that. How's your prayer life?"

I said, "Not as good as it should be."

A third guy said, "Here's what you should do. Get up a half an hour earlier. What time do you get up in the morning?" I told him 6:30 a.m. "Then why don't you get up at 6:00 and spend an extra half of an hour in the Word?"

I said, "Oh, you guys, you're not listening to me. I'm tired. I'm beat. I don't need this kind of advice."

They challenged me to get up a half hour earlier to spend time with the Lord. And I did it. I came back a month later, and the first thing they asked me was, "How did it go?"

I told them, "You helped me. God has been blessing me." Every leader needs this kind of accountability group.

Even the most seasoned believer has room to grow. Don't shy away from opportunities to learn from God through other Christians! Consider who you can ask to mentor you.

## YOUR WALK WITH GOD

Your personal, growing, living relationship with God is the basis for your mentoring relationships. If this area of your life is in shambles, take time to mend it before you pursue mentorship. While there are many areas of life that mentoring facilitates growth in, a person's relationship with God should be the area of major concern. As Jesus said, "For whoever wants to save his life will lose it, but whoever loses his life for me will find it. What good will it be for a man if he gains the whole world, yet forfeits his soul? Or what can a man give in exchange for his soul?" (Matthew 16:25-26).

Beverly Sallee is a caring, gifted, and committed woman. She has followers who love her all over the world. She ministers to every conceivable type of person (religion, creed, color, back-

> Your **personal**, **growing**, living relationship with **God** is the basis for your **mentoring** relationships.

ground, etc.). She says, "Ron Jenson told me that many people spend so much time caring for others or for their work that they let their own lives atrophy. That used to be me—serve everyone else and let myself dwindle down to the 'fumes.' Ron encouraged me to take time for myself, that it was necessary if I was to remain effective with so many responsibilities and people of so many different cultures. I have begun to apply that, and there is quite a difference." In a mentoring relationship, you are serving others. Therefore, it is essential that you do not let yourself "dwindle down to the fumes" in your relationship with God.

This book cannot fully cover the essentials to a relationship with God. For more information, see *Knowing God* by J. I. Packer, *Celebration of Discipline* by Richard Foster, or *The Sacred Romance* by Brent Curtis and John Eldredge.

## INSIGHTS FROM PAUL

First Corinthians 9:24–27 says:

> Do you not know that in a race all the runners run, but only one gets the prize? Run in such a way as to get the prize. Everyone who competes in the games goes into strict training. They do it to get a crown that will not last; but we do it to get a crown that will last forever. Therefore I do not run like a man running aimlessly; I do not fight like a man beating the air. No, I beat my body and make it my slave so that after I have preached to others, I myself will not be disqualified for the prize.

Paul took his responsibility seriously. If only one runner was to get the prize, Paul was determined to root out everything that would stand between him and that eternal prize. His body and desires did not have mastery over him. No, Paul says he would get in the boxing ring with his body in order to maintain control.

Initially there is nothing enjoyable about discipline because discipline involves pain. Anyone who is involved in the process of self-discipline experiences pain. Paul's illustration of beating his body means that we must bring virtually every part of our lives into submission through discipline in order that we might win the race of life and not be disqualified.

Self-discipline also requires perseverance. You need to persevere until discipline becomes a reality for you. If you are determined to harness God's power and focus it on that area (or areas) of your life that requires change, you will see change. The key to God's power to change you is your willingness to concentrate your efforts and stick with it until you have formed new habits and have gained self-discipline.

It is . . . essential that we commit to leading sinless, exemplary lives out of our love for God.

God's desire for us is that we develop positive habits and that we establish healthy routines that will help us lead a lifestyle that honors him. As mentors, we must lead self-disciplined lives of love and service for God. Our relationship with him will serve as the basis for our mentoree's growth. Therefore, it is all the more essential that we commit to leading sinless, exemplary lives out of our love for God.

*"Self-discipline defined as the 'correction or regulation of oneself for the sake of improvement,' raises the question, 'What is the fundamental root for self-discipline?' Is it self-determination? Is it simply to 'try harder'? Or is there a greater depth to self-discipline?*

*"The Bible suggests a healthy self-worth and worthy concept of God are necessary to render self-discipline. You must first have a healthy respect toward your Creator and then for yourself. As that 'great philosopher' once said, 'God don't make no junk.' In order for you to even attempt self-discipline and self-sacrifice, you must view yourself as God views you. Once you come to grips with your own value as God values you, your respect for your time and the time of others, your influence on business acquaintances and peers, and a healthy respect for God's holiness laws will all come into clear focus. That unwavering respect for the love of your spouse will protect you from the damages of unfaithfulness, and your steadfast desire for God-consciousness will enable you to overcome old habits that can derail your progressive sanctification.*

*"God wants you to be a self-motivated, self-assured, healthy person who will then be able to mentor others. Being a part of an accountability group can reinforce God's fashioning of your life and enable you to invest your life into the life of another—and that is fundamental to bibli-*

*cal self-discipline and self-sacrifice."*

—DONALD L. BRAKE, Ph.D., is dean of
Multnomah Biblical Seminary in
Portland, Oregon, and has been in educational
leadership for more than twenty-five years.

*"Over the years I have observed not only others' struggles, but also my own struggles in seeking to obtain self-discipline. I have steadily grown in two convictions. One, that the only race worthy of running with full devotion is to become a mature and equipped follower of Christ; and two, that the only way to become a mature and equipped follower of Christ is to run in such a way to win. Such running requires self-discipline. Whether you call it self-discipline or self-control, the dangerous word is 'self.' Though God has called us to control or discipline ourselves, such effort is possible only by the work of God's Spirit.*

*"One of the most important truths I have learned in life is that only to the degree that I acknowledge my own inability to change myself and focus on the ability of Christ alone to change me, can my 'fallen self' be controlled or disciplined. Without the work of God's Spirit, at best I can only change my actions. But true self-discipline is backed by pure motives and to do so must always take us to the cross. Without such focus, we begin to change ourselves 'in order' to have God's love instead of the proper motivation, 'because' I have God's love. Never forget Zachariah's words 'not by might, nor by power, but by my Spirit says the Lord of hosts' (4:6b)."*

—RANDY POPE is the teaching pastor at
Perimeter Church in Duluth, Georgia.

*"After college I spent the first eight years of my professional life in the United States Marine Corps. Early on we were taught that as a basic tenet of leadership, virtue and self-discipline truly and essentially separate one person from another. From the killing fields of Vietnam, thirty years ago, to the Chief Executive Officer's chair in a one and a half billion dollar company, that lesson remains valid. Without self-discipline all of the brains, inspiration, and education in the world will not get you past the starting gate of achievement. Without virtue and the self-discipline to pursue it, you will never know significance that only God can provide. Self-discipline is not the suffering and denial most people think. It is what enables you to achieve lifelong satisfaction that comes from the progressive and patient realization of worthy goals."*

—JIM AMOS, Jr., is the chairman and CEO of Sona MedSpa, the chairman emeritus of Mail Boxes Etc. (The UPS Store), past chairman of the International Franchise Association (IFA), chairman of MedVisits, and managing partner of Eagle Alliance Partners. He is the author of two books, *Focus or Failure: America at the Crossroads* and *The Memorial*. He is currently working on his third book, *The Idiot's Guide to Franchising*, to be published by Penguin Press in 2005.

*"To be a disciple is to be disciplined. The authors correctly note that discipline has both positive and negative aspects: saying 'Yes' to the good and saying 'No' to the bad. They remind us that discipline is not a once-for-all state of being, but a process, gained through a series of small but definite decisions, one on top of another.* Christian

discipline, they would agree, has Christ both as the motivator and the engine (with the Holy Spirit). As the writer of Hebrews says, 'let us also lay aside every weight, and sin which clings so closely, and let us run with endurance the race that is set before us, looking to Jesus, the founder and perfecter of our faith.'"

—STAN GUTHRIE is the senior associate news editor at Christianity Today. He is the author of *Missions in the Third Millennium*.

"The rewards of self-discipline are enlightening. At the start of last year, I had no new resolutions for myself. However my desire to help my daughters develop a certain habit made up a new 'resolution.'

"I decided to get both of my girls a devotional book for Christmas. I prayed about their discipline in actually using them. My girls are ten and twelve years old. That was my New Year's resolution . . . for them to have the discipline to have daily devotions.

"After the devotional books sat on their book shelves for what seemed like eternity, I knew it was going to take something different to get these girls going. I set my alarm a few minutes earlier than normal to wake up Rachael and Rebekah. I invited them to come and snuggle with me in my bed. As we snuggled, I suggested we have devotions. So I read the Scripture and the devotional, and we all prayed. This went on morning after morning. Now, most of the time, one of the girls reads the Scripture and the other one reads the devotional.

"One morning I was going to have an early morning business phone call. I told the girls the night before we *couldn't have devotions, and they both said, 'Mom, let's just get up a bit earlier.'*

*"There were certainly mornings I did not want to get up any earlier. I already had my set time for my own devotions. Having enough discipline to help others carve a new habit into their own lives comes from a strong foundation of self-discipline. We can best mentor others from the overflow of our own lives. If we want others to follow in our footsteps, we better know where our footsteps are going."*

—PAM LEONE serves as associate director of Young
Life's Capernaum Ministries.

*"Daily, each of us is confronted with the need to do something we don't prefer. If we can't exercise the self-discipline to do that, we contribute to the process of personal failure. Whether in choosing what is right in order to live the Christian life or what must be changed in order to grow personally, ultimate success is usually the culmination of many choices. Many of these choices require the self-discipline to say 'no' to feelings and 'yes' to God."*

—STEVE DOUGLASS serves as president of Campus
Crusade for Christ International.

### HOW ABOUT YOU?
Determine your level of proficiency in the area of self-discipline from the chart below. 1 is the lowest, 10 is the highest with 5 as average.

## SELF-DISCIPLINE

| 1 | 1.5 | 2 | 2.5 | 3 | 3.5 | 4 | 4.5 | 5 | 5.5 | 6 | 6.5 | 7 | 7.5 | 8 | 8.5 | 9 | 9.5 | 10 |
|---|-----|---|-----|---|-----|---|-----|---|-----|---|-----|---|-----|---|-----|---|-----|----|

What do you need to do in order to improve half of a point this week in your mentoring relationships?

*"Nothing is so strong as gentleness, and nothing is so gentle as real strength."*

-RALPH W. SOCKMAN

*"If you are kind, people may accuse you of selfish, ulterior motives. Be kind anyway. . . . You see, in the final analysis, it is between you and God. It was never between you and them anyway."*

-MOTHER TERESA

# Chapter 3

# GENTLENESS

**M**entoring is often long, hard work. Mentors who expect to see quick results and perfect lives should reconsider mentoring. The process requires people who are willing to be tender and patient over the long haul. A gentle touch will often have the largest impact and the best staying power. A gentle mentor will often have the best chance to change his mentoree and influence her life for good. Change in your mentoree's life will come through your loving gentleness.

First Thessalonians 2:6–12 gives us an example of godly gentleness in mentoring. The apostle Paul, Silas, and Timothy were gentle in their dealings with the Thessalonian church. This passage shows us the strength of their gentleness. It says:

> As apostles of Christ we could have been a burden to you, but we were gentle among you, like a mother caring for her little children. We loved you so much that we were delighted to share with you not only the gospel of God but our lives as well, because you had become so dear to us. Surely you remember, brothers, our toil and hardship; we worked night and day in order not to be

a burden to anyone while we preached the gospel of God to you.

You are witnesses, and so is God, of how holy, righteous and blameless we were among you who believed. For you know that we dealt with each of you as a father deals with his own children, encouraging, comforting, and urging you into his kingdom and glory.

Paul said they were "gentle . . . like a mother caring for her little children." The significance of this metaphor is that we are to be, in attitude and action, as a nursing mother tenderly caring for her child. That gentle love meant that Paul willingly shared his life and spent his energy for the Thessalonians. Though they could have used force, Paul, Timothy, and Silas acted like mothers with newborn children. The result was that the Thessalonian believers were a cause of thankfulness for they had love, faith, and hope in Jesus Christ (1 Thessalonians 1:2-3).

There are many myths concerning gentleness. Using Paul's words above, we will examine these myths and discover true qualities of gentleness as they relate to mentoring.

GENTLENESS IS NOT . . .

Gentleness is not passive ineffectiveness but tender, caring strength. There is often a negative connotation with the word gentleness. It tends to make people think of spineless people who easily give in to others' wishes. Its synonyms include mildness, calmness, and mellowness. Yet a father who delivers a strong warning to his son apart from the family reunion is exhibiting gentleness. So is a kind friend who chooses appropriate words to tell a friend disappointing news.

Gentleness is not skirting around the issue or giving up before the issue has been addressed. Instead, it involves a right attitude in handling the conflicts and issues that inevitably arise. A father shows gentleness in removing his son from a place of embarrassment or shame before warning him. He is also gentle in his physical and emotional messages to the son. With a calm voice and a kind hand, he communicates the hard message while protecting his son with his gentle strength. A gentle mentor speaks tender, thoughtful words and does not seek to shame or humiliate her mentoree.

**Gentleness is not passive ineffectiveness but tender, caring strength.**

Gentleness is not weakness. Paul, Timothy, and Silas had suffered and been insulted yet they gently moved forward with their mission: to declare the gospel in spite of strong opposition. Knowing that they were following God, not bowing to men's threats, they showed no weakness. They could not give up on their quest, but they also would not fight back (1 Thessalonians 2:2). In pursuit of the best for your protégé, you will need to couple determination with gentle strength.

Gentleness is not ineffectiveness. Although Paul talks of love, suffering, and servant living, he assures the Thessalonians that, as they know, the visit to them "was not a failure" (1 Thessalonians 2:1). In fact, their "faith in God [had] become known everywhere" (1:8), and they "accepted the word of God, which you heard from us (Paul,

Timothy, and Silas) . . . not as the word of men, but as it actually is, the word of God" (2:13). Paul and his coworkers achieved their objectives with the people God had sent them to work with (their mentorees) through gentleness.

Gentleness is not a lack of confidence or assertiveness. Rather, gentleness from God gives you a cool-headed ability to assert the truth and confidently stand for what is right. Paul says, "But with the help of our God we dared to tell you his gospel in spite of strong opposition" (1 Thessalonians 2:2). Asserting and confidently standing for what is right will allow your mentoree to rely on your gentle stand for truth.

> **Gentleness** from God gives you a cool-headed **ability** to **assert** the truth and confidently stand for what is **right**.

Gentleness is not false flattery. Nor is it covering over the truth. "A gentle answer turns away wrath" (Proverbs 15:1) does not mean that the answer is diluted or false. It means that the answer is given in a gentle manner. When Paul says "You know we never used flattery, nor did we put on a mask to cover up greed—God is our witness" (1 Thessalonians 2:5), he is not saying that they only spoke harsh words which did not flatter the listening Thessalonian church. Instead, he is saying that their words, their actions, and their motives were based on gentle selflessness that both God and the Thessalonian church could attest to. Can your mentoree attest to such gentleness?

Gentleness is certainly not passivity. A gentle person does not shy away from responsibility, including responsibility to speak and act rightly in the life of another. Paul says, "For the appeal we make does not spring from error or impure motives, nor are we trying to trick you. On the contrary, we speak as men approved by God to be entrusted with the gospel. We are not trying to please men but God, who tests our hearts" (1 Thessalonians 2:3–4). Paul's words from God were not passively set aside because they might offend. Instead, Paul and his fellow workers knew that they must gently speak all that God has instructed because they were trying to please him, not other people.

Gentleness is often misunderstood and misrepresented. Now that we know what gentleness is not, let's look at what gentleness *is*.

GENTLENESS IS . . .

Gentleness is need-oriented. When Queen Esther saw the critical need for her input in order to save her people, the Jews, she stepped in and made gentle requests of her non-Jewish husband, King Xerxes. A hasty, abrupt demand would have probably cost her life. She chose to gently bring the matter before the king in such a way that he could not refuse her request. She saw the need that only she could fill, and she rose up to meet it gently.

Gentleness is tender. Two good examples of tender gentleness are the founders of Zondervan Publishing. As I (Ted) completed my college career, I applied to a number of Christian book publishing firms for a position in the publishing world. In response to one of my applications, I was invited by two gentlemen to come to Grand Rapids,

> Gentleness is **need-oriented** and **tender**.

Michigan, to be interviewed for a position with the newly formed Zondervan Publishing House. The two brothers, who were to become two of my closest friends and my earliest mentors, were P. J. (Pat) and B. D. (Bernie) Zondervan. I joined the staff as a junior editor and in the ensuing dozen years was promoted to senior editor as well as manager of the advertising, promotion, and production divisions of the corporation.

I learned so much from these two very gifted entrepreneurs. They took me under their wings and introduced me to the significant world of Christian publications. I learned from them the vital importance of integrity. Every transaction in the company was open and above board in every aspect; they never cut corners but insisted that every business transaction be fair and equitable. I learned from them the importance of documenting all decisions by means of memoranda for future reference and accountability. The two brothers taught me the importance of praying over vital business decisions. They modeled gentleness through treating every employee, vender, and author with utmost respect.

I worked there for twelve years, and I really learned the art of deal making with authors and how to interview prospective authors. One of the first manuscripts I worked on was an English translation of Kierkegaard's theology. I learned at Zondervan the art of tactful approach with other publishers. We were competing with old time publishers, and we were new. I learned that each individual had to be treated like a separate personality. We checked what their likes and dislikes were. We had to take in some established authors and encourage the new authors who wanted to get into print.

My family became well acquainted with the gentleness of Pat and Bernie and their families. We traveled with them a great deal and found that they were men of integrity above everything else (we traveled largely for author contacts). We spent hours together in conferences with authors; we traveled widely together making contacts, and I never saw them lose their poise or equilibrium.

In our twelve years of close association, they did not seemingly attempt to enter into a mentoring relationship with me, but I learned so much simply by watching them in action. In later years I often thought back to my experiences with them and reflected on the lessons learned in watching them guide what became the leading Christian book publishing organization in the nation.

Zondervan was my training that God provided for my future leadership responsibilities. They modeled what they taught, that every individual is different, and you can't characterize people. You have to meet them on common ground. I had thought when I entered the publishing world that I would spend a lifetime in the field, yet I left the organization to be identified with the leadership of Youth for Christ International when I was strangely prompted by the Holy Spirit. The Zondervan brothers were not resentful but wished me well as I accepted God's call and faced a major and drastic change in my career. Even after I left the company, we remained close friends. Their tender gentleness allowed me to flourish under their direction and to follow God's best wherever it took me.

Gentleness is patient. This is probably best seen in Jesus' dealings with those who came to him. The woman who had bled for twelve years and who had suffered a great deal came to Jesus to be healed. Jesus could have been in a hurry to get to the house of Jairus, the synagogue ruler, in order to heal his little daughter who was dying. Yet, Jesus stopped in the crowd when he felt the sick woman touch his cloak and receive healing. He said to her, "Daughter, your faith has healed you. Go in peace and be freed from your suffering." His gentle patience made the difference between sickness and health for that woman (see Luke 8:40–56).

## GENTLE SUGGESTIONS

Mentors need to help protégés to discover and practice patterns and methods that work best for them. It takes gentleness to be able to offer suggestions and motivate positive habits. Depending on your mentoree's personality, it is usually best to give *options* in a particular situation, rather than instruct her on what she must do (the exception is in cases of blatant sin in which there are not multiple legitimate options).

> Mentors need to help **protégés** to discover and practice **patterns** and methods that **work best** for them.

JoAnn Bengel says, "I can turn to my mentor when I am facing a difficult decision and know that I will not be told what to do, but will receive options and choices to help me make the best possible choice. That is what a mentor does. A mentor listens to the person's issue or life questions, weighs the options, and makes suggestions. A mentor keeps you accountable for your walk with Christ, relationships with others and spouse, but does not tell you what you should be doing."

A mentor keeps his protégé on the right track when making decisions but doesn't demand that things be done the way he wants. This is when a mentoring relationship needs depth. If you don't know your mentoree's strengths and weaknesses, then you will have trouble directing and motivating her in positive directions. The more that you understand the way she works and the past choices that have or have not worked out as planned, the more effective you can be in the future.

> A mentor keeps his protégé on the **right track** when making decisions but **doesn't** demand that things be done the way he **wants.**

## GENTLE LOVE

Gentleness. That is the first word that comes to mind when I think of my (Ron) dad. My dad delivered—big time. He wrestled with me and my brother on the living room floor. He always came to my football, baseball, and basketball games.

He was patient with me when I was a pain in the neck, which was the norm during my pre-teen years. I never heard him raise his voice in anger. Instead, he encouraged, loved, built up, and praised me and my siblings.

It's his *character* that makes me proud of him—his work ethic, his love and compassion, his sensitivity, his integrity, his faithfulness and intelligence, but most of all, his gentleness. Because he was gentle with me, a foundation was masterfully laid for the Holy Spirit's work in my life.

My dad's love was a gentle love that considered my needs and rose to meet them, all without being pushy or self-centered. His gentle heart mirrored my heavenly Father's gentle love. That love graciously allows us to have endless new starts and clean slates.

In your mentoring relationships, do not neglect to lay a foundation of gentle care for your mentoree. Through your gentle strength and sensitive suggestions, your mentoree will have the tools to become more efficient in the workplace, the church, and the home.

A gentle attitude may take time to develop. Commit to being tender and patient in all of your relationships, especially with those people that you desire to impact. A gentle touch in your protégé's life will help bring about change that will last.

### OTHER LEADERS SAY . . .

*"The sports world is not known for its tenderness and gentility. Too often, those who coach the ones who compete think they must use coercion, anger, and retribution to instill a winning spirit in their charges. However, we have an example of one man—a classy Christian man—who proved that gentleness can lead to sports success, just as it can lead to success in all other mentoring relationships.*

*"John Wooden, the venerable coach of the UCLA Bruins when they won ten NCAA basketball championships, was a gentleman in every way. He never yelled. He never threw things. He never berated his players. Instead, with gentle, wise, and thoughtful words and actions, he molded his players into championship teams. Today, they look back with fondness and utmost respect to their old coach. Wooden is a grand example of mentoring for success while*

*displaying the kinds of Christlike gentleness and meek-*
*ness that Ted Engstrom and Ron Jenson described in this*
*chapter."*

—DAVE BRANON is the managing editor of
Sports Spectrum magazine and is a contributing
writer for *Our Daily Bread*. He is the author of thirteen
books, including the *Sports Devotional Bible* and
*Heads Up!*, a sports-related devotional for kids.
Dave and his wife, Sue, have four children and live in
Grand Rapids, Michigan.


*"Being afflicted with a rather 'driven' personality type,*
*I gaze over the fence longingly at other Christian men,*
*especially those in leadership, who exhibit gentleness. By*
*some alchemy they manage to get as much, or more, done*
*than I do, and yet do it in a gentle manner. This year I*
*delivered a funeral message at the service for my mentor*
*pastor. He impacted my life and ministry for over two*
*decades.*

*"What was the essence of this man? Aside from the obvi-*
*ous things, like unswerving commitment to the Scriptures*
*and a love for the lost, he was a consummate gentleman*
*with an accent on the word, 'gentle.' He never scolded me,*
*although I certainly gave him reason to do so at times. I*
*never witnessed him treat anyone with unkindness. He*
*treated his wife like a princess. His grade-school daughter*
*snuggled to his side as they sat in church and told me he*
*was her hero. I learned much from this man, but the most*
*important facet of leadership I learned from him, which*
*he never told to me, only showed to me, was the inesti-*
*mable value of being a 'gentle-man' to the church board,*
*to the weak and hurting, to the custodian, to the secretar-*

*ies, to the congregation, to vendors, to anyone God put in his path, and even to his adversaries.*

*"And when he died, the place was packed; because people knew this man loved them. And I miss him. I miss his affectionate squeeze on my arm. I miss his quiet words of affirmation after every sermon he ever heard me preach. I miss him introducing me to his peers as his true 'Timothy.' I miss him asking about my wife and kids. I've forgotten almost all his sermons, but I'll never forget his gentleness."*

—TIM WALTON is the founding pastor of Snohomish Community Church northeast of Seattle. He has been a pastor for thirty-two years, and punctuates ministry with running and mountain climbing. He's been married thirty years and has four children, with the youngest serving in the U.S. Army.

*"I agree wholeheartedly that a mentor needs to be gentle and patient over the long haul in order to encourage and build up the mentoree and effect change that is lasting. It is vitally important, therefore, that the character of a mentor be deeply rooted in Christ—in order for gentleness to be consistent and authentic. All people, mentors and mentorees alike, are spiritually depraved. As a follower of Christ, through dependence on him alone, the mentor develops a gentle and loving attitude. As a gentle attitude grows, it allows the mentor to mirror our heavenly Father's gentle love. When this Christ-like love is coupled with deep respect for the mentoree, the mentoree can rise above both the mentor's expectations and their own.*

*"The mentor needs to remember to follow Jesus' example of gentleness, to trust the Lord for the fruit of the Spirit, and to abide in Christ and allow him to work in his or her life as a mentor. The fruit of the spirit needs to be evident in the mentor's life, so that the mentor can lead by example and patiently point the way to Christ, which will produce lasting fruit in the mentoree's life. Being a gentle mentor is a privilege and provides a double blessing for eternity—it gives the mentor the opportunity of personal growth in Christ, while investing in the mentoree's life, one step at a time."*

—MARIE HERSETH KENOTE, DMA, is an assistant professor of music at Nyack College as well as a freelance flutist. She lives in New Jersey with her husband and three daughters.

*"As a former NFL player, I have experienced some very harsh and unkind mentoring over my life, and I have received some very appropriate and gentle mentoring. About fourteen years ago my wife, Bobbe, and I were going through a very difficult time in our marriage. My mentor suggested that harshness and unkindness were wrong to a follower of Jesus Christ because they are opposite of what God wants to display in my life (Gal. 5:22). He told me to ask God to remind me every time I displayed the opposite of gentleness and kindness toward Bobbe. I made it my goal to be gentle with her in every situation for the next year. I was amazed at the changes that came about in our relationship. That choice helped restore our marriage to a healthy relationship. God will provide gentleness and kindness in you if you choose to allow him to provide it through you."*

—NORM EVANS is the president of Pro Athletes
Outreach, whose mission is to equip pro athletes,
coaches, and their families to make a positive impact.

*"For fun I looked up* gentle *in my thesaurus and found
words like kind, gracious, considerate, thoughtful,
merciful, and compassionate. I love these words. They
resonate within my soul and describe how I long to have
people respond to me when I need encouragement and
direction.*

*"Looking back through the years of my spiritual journey,
the people who have influenced me the most are the ones
who guided me with tender patience. They didn't push or
pull, but held my hand and walked alongside of me no
matter how long or how hard the journey.*

*"Perhaps these words written by an unknown author say
it best: A friend is someone who knows you as you are,
understands where you've been, accepts who you've become and still, gently invites you to grow."*

—ALICE GRAY is an inspirational speaker and
award-winning author. She's the author of
*Treasures for Women Who Hope.*

*"As I reflect on this chapter, the word picture of gentle-
ness that strikes me the most is 'like a mother caring for
her little children.' Being the mother of three, perhaps that
is why I can readily and easily relate to that image. But
it is the remembrance of my own mother's gentleness that
really comes to mind. When my sisters and I get together,
we spend hours retelling and laughing about the many
lectures and repeated 'mom-isms' we received and shared*

*over the years. But the lessons I remember most from my mother are not from words, but from her actions—her tender strength in guiding me through the pain of rejection; her patient listening when I poured out my heart; her loving acceptance of me no matter how big a mistake I had made.*

*"It was those lessons of gentleness that have shaped and guided my own attitudes and behaviors with my children. Gentleness of spirit is often overlooked as a positive quality. But a truly gentle person is a rarity: a gem valued above all others. Gentleness is not easy—to be tender, yet strong; to listen and not be judgmental; to be compassionate yet not withhold the truth. That is the challenge, but one well worth the effort."*

> —BETSY SCHMITT serves as project editor for the Livingstone Corporation in Carol Stream, Illinois.

*"Reading this chapter reminds me that being a 'gentleman' is a concept from a bygone era. Today, if a man shows too much kindness and sensitivity he runs the risk of being called a 'girlie-man.' Being gentle isn't in. Most people still believe that 'nice guys finish last.' That's why this chapter seems so counter-cultural.*

*"Humanity has always believed that the strong, the warriors, even the cruel, are the winners. Jesus proved otherwise. When the enemies of Christ entered the garden to arrest him, carrying swords and clubs, he faced them as a true gentleman. Peter, on the other hand, was ready to fight. Swinging wildly, he trimmed off someone's ear. Jesus, in an act of true gentleness, picked up the severed ear and healed it.*

*"Even when falsely accused, Jesus was gentle like a lamb. He was treated harshly by Jewish leaders, mocked by Herod, brutalized by Roman soldiers, finally bludgeoned and nailed to a rough wooden post. We lose our gentleness when someone cuts us off in traffic. But Jesus remained gentle until the end, even expressing compassion for his enemies.*

*"As the darkness fell, it seemed that cruelty had won. The gentle One, who wouldn't break a bruised reed, seemed to have been broken and crushed by his foes. It seemed that the nicest guy had finished last after all. But, in the most amazing reversal of human history, Jesus Christ turned the tables. He rose again and 'having disarmed the powers and authorities, he made a public spectacle of them, triumphing over them by the cross' (Col. 2:15).*

*"Gentleness won! And ever since the triumph of Christ, men and women of gentleness have proven its power to conquer evil and transform the human race. From Nazi concentration camps, to the ghettos of New York, to the slums of Calcutta, gentleness has triumphed.*

*"As Ralph W. Sockman said, 'Nothing is so strong as gentleness, and nothing is so gentle as real strength.' The kind of gentleness taught in this chapter takes great courage. It requires real strength of character to go against the cultural current and natural human tendencies. It's tough to be tender. But Jesus, Paul, and a courageous multitude of believers since have shown that true gentleness has the potential to change the world. Count me in."*

—JOHN SAWYER is a partner in Grey Matter Group, a marketing firm that specializes in branding and communication for Christian organizations. He has seen the power of gentleness firsthand in some of the Christian leaders he has had the privilege of serving with at organizations like Zondervan, World Vision, Open Doors, LPEA, MOPS, and Baker Publishing Group.

## HOW ABOUT YOU?

Determine your level of proficiency in the area of gentleness from the chart below. 1 is the lowest, 10 is the highest with 5 as average.

**GENTLENESS**

| 1 | 1.5 | 2 | 2.5 | 3 | 3.5 | 4 | 4.5 | 5 | 5.5 | 6 | 6.5 | 7 | 7.5 | 8 | 8.5 | 9 | 9.5 | 10 |
|---|---|---|---|---|---|---|---|---|---|---|---|---|---|---|---|---|---|---|

What do you need to do in order to improve half of a point this week in your mentoring relationships?

*"To love Christ is to love the people for whom he died, regardless of the risks."*

–TED W. ENGSTROM


*"To love another person is to help them love God."*

–SOREN KIERKEGAARD

# Chapter 4

# AFFECTION

W hen my (Ron) son, Matt, was in high school, we went to Promise Keepers together, and he came away with a vision for ministry in his school. During his senior year of high school, he was elected to the homecoming court. He was not an athletic star or a student body officer. I believe that he was chosen by his classmates because of his godly impact at school.

My wife, Mary, and I went to the homecoming game to participate in the crowning ceremony with Matt. There were thousands of people in the stands that night. At halftime, Mary and I, along with other parents of court members, were supposed to go down the fifty-yard line with our children. At that point, they would name the king and queen.

Matt was in a tuxedo, and as we approached him, he reached out and took his mother's hand. Then, he reached out like he wanted to hold my hand. I thought, "You don't want to do this. There are a lot of people here and they might see us holding hands. I don't want them to think that my son is a wimp." So I put my hand in my pocket and walked next to him. We went elbow in elbow down the sideline, and he was named the homecoming king.

The next day, Mary came to me and said, "Do you know how much you hurt your son last night?"

I was shocked and said, "No, I don't. What do you mean?"

She told me that Matt wanted to hold my hand and walk hand-in-hand down the fifty yard line. I wondered why. She said, "So many of these kids, teachers, parents, and administrators know him, and they know how close he is to his family, especially his dad. He wanted to show them that closeness, but you robbed him of that opportunity. You'll never get it back."

I felt awful, and I profusely apologized to Matt. He was gracious and forgave me. That night at the football game, I had let the world's "John Wayne" macho mindset get me. Instead of being affectionate with my son, I let the culture push me into a mode.

We need to affectionately love people, especially those we mentor. Paul says in 1 Thessalonians 2:8, "We loved you so much that we were delighted to share with you not only the gospel of God but our lives as well, because you had become so dear to us." Can you sense the intensity of feeling that Paul had for these people?

Bible scholars say that the phrase "loved you so much," which occurs only once in the whole New Testament, means a "warm, inward attachment" or "to feel oneself drawn to something or someone with intense longing" (Kittle and Friedrich, *Theological Dictionary of the New Testament*).

Furthermore, the words translated "so dear" are found several times throughout the New Testament and are often translated "dearly beloved." Paul not only says that they had a fond affection for these people, but that their ministry flowed out of the fact that these people had become greatly loved by Paul, Timothy, and Silas.

While other traits of a mentor are practical, affection for your protégé is largely emotional. It is practically worked out, but its foundation is in the feelings and convictions of the mentor.

**Affection is practically worked out, but its foundation is in the feelings and convictions of the mentor.**

The concept of an affectionate and significantly emotional attachment to other people is a pattern that runs throughout all of Scripture. All we need to do is look at such passages as Genesis 45:14-15 when Joseph "threw his arms around his brother Benjamin and wept, and Benjamin embraced him, weeping. And he (Joseph) kissed all his brothers and wept over them." This was all during their emotional reunion after years of broken relationships.

First Samuel 16:1 describes the prophet Samuel intensely mourning because God had rejected Saul as king. First Samuel 20:41 tells of David's and Jonathan's relationship which involved such strong emotions as grief and intense love.

In the Gospel of Luke, we read of the woman who poured a jar of perfume on Jesus' feet and wiped them with her hair (7:38-39). Her love for Jesus was manifested through her affectionate touch and self-sacrifice. Acts 20:37-38 records the intense feelings that the Ephesian elders had for the apostle Paul; they wept at the thought of never seeing him again.

Finally, Romans 16:16 instructs the Roman church to "Greet one another with a holy kiss." Affection has a set place in Scripture. It is easy to see the intense caring and genuine affection that God's people shared in Bible times. The same care and affection is greatly needed and equally appropriate in your mentoring relationships today as well.

THINK AFFECTIONATELY

Focus on your mentoree's strengths in your thoughts of her. Our thoughts dictate our words and our actions. Jesus said, "The good man brings good things out of the good stored up in his heart, and the evil man brings evil things out of the evil stored up in his heart. For out of the overflow of his heart his mouth speaks" (Luke 6:45).

> Focus on your mentoree's strengths. . . . Our thoughts dictate our words and our actions.

One of the easiest ways to abort affection for someone is to entertain negative emotions such as anger, unforgiveness and bitterness. Such feelings must be conquered if we are to lead a successful Christian life: "But now you must rid yourselves of all such things as these: anger, rage, malice, slander, and filthy language from your lips" (Colossians 3:8). Later on, in Colossians 3:12–14, Paul says:

> Therefore, as God's chosen people, holy and dearly loved, clothe yourselves with compassion, kindness, humility, gentleness and patience. Bear with each other and forgive whatever grievances you may have

against one another. Forgive as the Lord forgave you. And over all these virtues put on love, which binds them all together in perfect unity.

## SPEAK AFFECTIONATELY

Affirmation is the most obvious way to verbally share your affection. Refer to chapter 1 for tips on giving compliments and encouragement to your mentorees.

A less obvious way to express verbal affection is by keeping confidentiality. A mentoring relationship must be built on trust. Your protégé expects that the words spoken in your presence will be kept confidential. You can express affection and respect for your mentoree when you honor him by not sharing with others what you know about him.

If you do betray your mentoree's confidence, be honest. Tell him that you were wrong and that you will not do it again (and then follow through!). Ask for his forgiveness and commit again to keeping utmost confidentiality.

## ACT AFFECTIONATELY

Ministry flows out of a deep care for those you are ministering to. When we care for people, we are quick to meet their needs and help them in any way we can. Your relationship with your mentoree is built on your words but also on your actions. Show your mentoree that you love him through your actions.

> Ministry flows out of a deep care for those you are ministering to.

While our tendency may be to look at other people's weaknesses, we will never have a deep affection for them until we zero in on their strengths. In fact, did you know that your impact in life is in significant proportion to the sweetness of your spirit reflected through a positive tongue? That's right. Your impact on others has a great deal to do with a sweet, positive, upbeat attitude and tongue.

Philippians 2:14-16 illustrates this, "Do everything without complaining or arguing, so that you may become blameless and pure, children of God without fault in a crooked and depraved generation, in which you shine like stars in the universe as you hold out the word of life." These verses demonstrate the profound impact of your tongue to the world around you. Our word of life and our blameless lives will shine as bright as the stars if we refrain from complaining and arguing, that is, negative words.

Ted sometimes drops me (Ron) a note or gives me a call to say how proud he is of me and to encourage me. His affection for me is a powerful extension of biblical love. Biblical love is an unfettered, free love that releases the one loved to be the best that they can be.

Biblical love is seen in God's love affair with his people down through history. You can't escape that kind of love. Let's explore this by looking at a few passages about God's love for us and his call for us to love others, especially those we mentor.

## THE GREATEST COMMANDMENT

When asked what the greatest commandment in the law was, Jesus replied, "Love the Lord your God with all your heart and with all your soul and with all your mind." How is this lived out in the mentoring relationship?

In this context, Christ gave his disciples "a new commandment," a challenge to love one another as he had demonstrated. This was the recurring theme of the Master as he prepared to leave his devoted followers. He called it the highest expression of discipleship, easily recognized, often hard to embrace, but proof that a person characterized by love was indeed a follower of The Way. The apostle John gives nearly a third of his gospel to the Lord's crowning theme—love—in the final days of his mission on earth.

## A MOST EXCELLENT WAY

Love is described in 1 Corinthians 13 as patient, kind, humble, selfless, polite, joyful in truth, hopeful, and persevering. This love is not compartmental love that selects sections or specifics to love, nor is it feelings-based love. This love is a way of life.

Anne Sire Greenquist shares about her mentor, Beverly Sallee, and the affection Beverly has for her, "I am always full of energy and full of belief in myself and in Christ when we depart. Me—the person that God created and gave so many gifts and has so many plans for; not the me where I see all my faults, and the me where I need many more gifts to feel valuable, even worth spending time with." Beverly gives Anne a sense of worth and value in the kingdom of God. Beverly's affection for Anne allows her to become the woman God created her to be.

Consider that Paul told the Thessalonian believers that he and his companions loved them so much and that they were so dear to them. Paul verbalized their affection. He spoke lovingly and uplifted them through his kind words, and so must we if we are going to be good mentors.

James 3:1-12 says:

> Not many of you should presume to be teachers, my brothers, because you know that we who teach will be judged more strictly. We all stumble in many ways. If anyone is never at fault in what he says, he is a perfect man, able to keep his whole body in check.
>
> When we put bits into the mouths of horses to make them obey us, we can turn the whole animal. Or take ships for example. Although they are so large and are driven by strong winds, they are steered by a very small rudder wherever the pilot wants to go. Likewise, the tongue is a small part of the body, but it makes great boasts. Consider what a great forest is set on fire by a small spark. The tongue also is a fire, a world of evil among the parts of the body. It corrupts the whole person, sets the whole course of his life on fire, and is itself set on fire by hell.
>
> All kinds of animals, birds, reptiles, and creatures of the sea are being tamed and have been tamed by man, but no man can tame the tongue. It is a restless evil, full of deadly poison.

With the tongue we praise our Lord and Father, and with it we curse men, who have been made in God's likeness. Out of the same mouth come praise and cursing. My brothers, this should not be. Can both fresh water and salt water flow from the same spring? My brothers, can a fig tree bear olives, or a grapevine bear figs? Neither can a salt spring produce fresh water.

Your mouth may be the biggest indicator of your character. It shows where your heart lies and where your priorities are. Matthew 12:34 says, "For out of the overflow of the heart the mouth speaks." What does your speech say is flowing out of your heart?

**Your mouth may be the biggest indicator of your character. It shows where your heart lies and where your priorities are.**

## FORGIVENESS

Total forgiveness is absolutely essential if we are going to have a positive feeling of committed affection within our mentoring relationships. Scripture says in Colossians 3:13 that as Christ forgave us, so we should forgive others. How did Jesus Christ forgive us? Totally! The Bible says that as a result of our accepting Jesus Christ as our Savior and Lord, "Their sins and lawless acts I will remember no more" (Hebrews 10:17).

The Old Testament promises, "As far as the east is from the west, so far has he removed our transgressions from us" (Psalm 103:12) and "'Come now, let us reason together,' says the LORD. 'Though your sins are like scarlet, they shall be as white as snow; though they are red as crimson, they shall be like wool'" (Isaiah 1:18).

Jesus Christ has totally and completely forgiven us. Therefore, we are to totally and completely forgive other people. We do not forgive because we are simply trying to be nice, but because we ourselves have already been forgiven by Jesus Christ.

What is complete and total forgiveness? If I forgive, three things are true. First, I never dwell on that sin again. If my protégé has sinned against me, I must consciously choose not to dwell on the issue again if I am truly to forgive him. Although the sin may come to mind sometimes, you must *will* to turn from it immediately. It will take commitment to not dwell on it.

> We do not **forgive** because we are simply trying to be **nice**, but because we ourselves have already **been forgiven** by Jesus Christ.

Second, total forgiveness means that I will never again talk to anybody else about the forgiven offense. How often we are tempted to talk behind people's backs! When you forgive someone, though, you pledge to never speak to anyone about what he or she did to you. You promise to keep your mouth shut when it comes to negative feelings. Rather than spilling negativity, you commit to speak positively about that person.

Third, you agree not to bring up the offense to the offender again. If you totally forgive, the offense is wiped away. It is as though he had never offended you at all. You cannot bring up the offense, either verbally or nonverbally; you must let it rest once and for all.

Last, don't expect future failure on the part of the offender. There is wisdom in re-adjusting expectations and levels of trust in response to sin. But forgiveness does not resign with the thought, "oh, well, they'll just do it again!" Set appropriate boundaries, and then set up your mentoree to succeed.

Does this all sound too difficult? Remember Jesus' words, "For if you forgive men when they sin against you, your heavenly Father will also forgive you. But if you do not forgive men their sins, your Father will not forgive your sins." We draw our strength to forgive completely and totally from our heavenly Father who forgave us of wrongs that are deeper than any we have received from others.

> Though we may not know what to pray for in specific situations . . . we can be sure that God always desires for his people to exhibit the fruits of a Spirit-filled life.

## PRAY AFFECTIONATELY

We must think affectionately, act affectionately, and speak affectionately. The final way that we can show affection for our mentorees is by positively praying for them.

When considering your desires for your mentoree, pray for positive, godly traits to become a part of his life. Refer to the fruits of the Spirit: love, joy, peace, patience, kindness, goodness, faithfulness, gentleness, and self-control (Galatians 5:22-23). Though we may not know what to pray for in specific situations in our mentoree's lives, we can be sure that God always desires for his people to exhibit the fruits of a Spirit-filled life.

## AFFECTIONATE LOVE

In an interview for the *Harvard Business Review*, Donald S. Perkins, head of the Jewel Companies, was asked whether he expected mentors to get emotionally involved with protégés. Perkins replied, "If you are asking me if you can work with people without love, the answer is no."

As mentors, we need to truly care for our mentorees and show them that affection through affirmation and positive words. Our affection has the ability to change their lives! Take the challenge to consciously think, act, speak, and pray in an affectionate manner in all of your mentoring relationships.

### OTHER LEADERS SAY . . .

*"Affection kindles the fire of positive energy that keeps the sun shining on very dark and discouraging days. When one's affections are energized by the love of another the darkness often turns to light. Mentors find that receiving love from a protégé can fan the flame of significance for the protégé. The mutuality of love strengthens the one who gives and the one who receives. Maturing relationships share a love that goes in two directions. You will find in mentoring relationships that when the mentor receives affection from the protégé she is really giving, not getting. My experience tells me that when I receive affection from my protégé, he finds deep significance. Affection has the capacity to receive, as well as to give."*

—DR. TIM ROBNETT serves as director of the
Luis Palau Evangelistic Association's
Next Generation Alliance ministries.

*"Affection—loving and being loved—doesn't come natu-*
*rally to many of us; it certainly doesn't to me. On the*
*other hand, I would have to admit that I experienced, by*
*far, the most personal growth those times when I was*
*dragged—kicking and screaming—into mentoring relation-*
*ships that would be described by Drs. Engstrom and Jen-*
*son as 'affectionate.'*

*"I can remember being taken under the wings of one men-*
*tor, a missionary on furlough from a country where people*
*just naturally and appropriately embraced and expressed*
*affection normally. He and his approach to discipleship*
*were somewhat unnerving to me—in some ways threaten-*
*ing. Looking back though, I would have to say that it is*
*the men who were men enough to be affectionate, patient,*
*and vulnerable who have most deeply shaped my life as a*
*pastor and evangelist.*

*"Dr. Engstrom and Dr. Jenson are right. There is no*
*biblical mentoring that is unaffectionate. Instead, in*
*Christ, we should be experiencing and exhibiting a*
*radical alien spiritual love. 'By this, they shall know*
*that you love me . . .' said Jesus. Step one for me as*
*a mentor desiring to be affectionate is to repent of my*
*self-focused hard heart that is unaffectionate by na-*
*ture. Step two for me is to quickly run to Christ again*
*and drink freely of his love and affection—his forgive-*
*ness and patience. Step three is then to go and love. It*
*doesn't get any better than this.*

—REV. BILL SENYARD is the pastor of Peace Valley
Community Church in Chalfont, Pennsylvania
(www.pvcsquared.org) and is one of the founders of the

postmodern gathering The Sanctuary in Doylestown. He is a popular author and conference speaker on the topics of identity, sexuality, justice, and forgiveness. He and his wife, Eunice, live in Doylestown with their three children.

*"I couldn't agree more with the authors. While serving our last church, there were fifteen retired pastors and missionaries in the congregation. Since we were in our early thirties, their presence had potential to be daunting or delightful. As it played out, those kind people and their spouses took turns showering my wife, Sue, and me with love and support.*

*"Three come to mind in particular. Ken Backlund, a large-church pastor, took me fishing several times, swapping stories through tears in a setting that felt like a father-son outing. Maurice Vanderburg, a national leader in urban ministry, was one of the most transparent friends I've ever enjoyed. He changed my life over many coffee dates. Bill Yaeger, a mentor to scores of young pastors during his days at a huge church in Modesto, used to call me on occasional Mondays and say, "Keith, first of all, you're my pastor, but I love you like a son. Second, why did you let such and such happen yesterday? Third, in case I forgot to mention it, I love you. I love you like a son." His affection was so sincere that his critiques were always welcome.*

*"All three men were strong leaders, and none of them were shy about telling, and showing, how much they cared about me. As the authors suggest, their affection made bold statements about my worth and coaxed out my potential. Without their affection, frankly, I*

*might not have valued their inputs. In some cases, I might have dodged or deflected, or even resented them. Their affection won my reciprocal investment in the mentoring process. It also informs my approach to mentoring others."*

—KEITH POTTER is the senior pastor of Saratoga Federated Church in suburban San Jose. Keith mentors pastoral students as a member of the adjunct faculty at Fuller Theological Seminary. He is also an author and frequent speaker at Mt. Hermon Conference Center.

*"In medical schools today professors often warn doctors-in-training to avoid 'getting too involved' because of the emotional price tag. Therapists often hear the same warning. In short, instructors recommend providing care without feeling affection for patients. Yet Jesus' modeling and instruction differ significantly from such advice.*

*"Jesus said people would identify his disciples by their love for one another (John 13:35). That sets apart Christian mentoring from other kinds of teacher/learner relationships. In the latter, those mentored may sometimes feel as if they're someone's 'project.' Relationships can be more about gaining knowledge and improving character than about genuine love.*

*"The Mentor loved the disciple John, and the disciple was so sure of Jesus' love that when he described himself, he didn't say 'John, son of Zebedee,' or 'John, the fisherman,' or even a heady 'John, of the Lord's inner circle.' Rather, he called himself 'the disciple whom Jesus loved.'*

*"Christian mentoring involves entering into people's lives so fully that we feel their experiences—including their*

*pain—as our own. Rather than cheering up or advising those who weep, we weep with them (Rom. 12:15). And we long for them with the affection of Christ Jesus (Phil. 1:5). Mentoring that's distinctly Christian stands out from the rest because 'the goal of our instruction is love from a pure heart and a good conscience and a sincere faith' (1 Tim. 1:5)."*

> —SANDRA GLAHN, *ThM, teaches at Dallas Theological Seminary, where she is editor-in-chief of the award-winning magazine,* Kindred Spirit. *In addition, she has co-authored eight books including the CBA best selling medical thriller,* Lethal Harvest. *She is currently writing a women's Bible study series for AMG Publishers.*

## HOW ABOUT YOU?

Determine your level of proficiency in the area of affection from the chart below. 1 is the lowest, 10 is the highest with 5 as average.

**AFFECTION**

| 1 | 1.5 | 2 | 2.5 | 3 | 3.5 | 4 | 4.5 | 5 | 5.5 | 6 | 6.5 | 7 | 7.5 | 8 | 8.5 | 9 | 9.5 | 10 |
|---|-----|---|-----|---|-----|---|-----|---|-----|---|-----|---|-----|---|-----|---|-----|----|

What do you need to do in order to improve half of a point this week in your mentoring relationships?

*"Communication is a process (verbal and nonverbal) of sharing information with another person in such a way that the other person understands what you are saying."*

—NORM WRIGHT

*"The challenge is to move toward and develop the supernatural ability to communicate truth with such a kind spirit that your words become a channel for God's transforming power."*

—UNKNOWN

# Chapter 5

# COMMUNICATION

**P**erhaps you've seen comic strips poking fun at the "communication" between a husband and wife. The wife says one thing but the husband hears a totally different message. The reason these comics strike us as funny is because they are so close to home. We know the feeling of being misunderstood or misheard. It's a frustrating feeling and when it happens to you, you probably don't feel like it's funny.

Without clear communication, our world would fall apart. Personally, our marriages and friendships would disintegrate into messes of confusion. Globally, our way of living and succeeding would crumble.

In mentoring—as in any significant relationship—effective communication is the backbone. There is no room for sloppy or inaccurate communicating. Good communication is when the "picture" of what you are communicating is the same in the mind of the person you are speaking to as it is in your own mind. Though *you* may understand what you are saying, if the picture that is formed in the mind of the other person is

> In mentoring—as in any **significant** relationship—effective communication is the **backbone.**

not the same as the intended picture, then communication is not really taking place. Contrary to the simplicity of this definition, the act of communication can be incredibly tough.

William James has said that "The most immutable barrier in nature is between one man's thought and another." Someone else has said that "You will never know what I mean, and I'll never know exactly what you mean." There is a set of dynamics in the communication process that make this seemingly simple activity excruciatingly difficult. Let's explore the process of communication in the mentoring relationship.

## PERMISSION TO COMMUNICATE

I (Ron) was called in to a corporate setting to help the employees work through problems that were affecting productivity and stability in the company. First, we went around the group and performed an exercise to help me get to know them. Everyone shared three things that others did not know about them, two things they were good at and one thing they would change if they could. Asking one question of the person to our left, we made our way around the circle. This helped the group loosen up and look at things differently.

After our exercise, I asked the question, "What is one thing you are going to do in light of the problem?" The CEO said, "I'm so frustrated now because we need to get away from this culture of fear and this repressive culture of micro-managing. I've been in my position four months and everyone is afraid to fail. I don't know if it's the culture or if it's me or if it's just the problems of the past, but it's driving me crazy." After this, the rest of the group shared about different things.

I wanted to get back to the CEO's statement so I said, "The CEO made this statement. He doesn't know what the problem is and no one answered him. I want to know: is your fear and lack of initiation a muscle-memory problem (the past) or what?" At this point, the employees talked honestly with the CEO about what the problems were. They couldn't talk until they were given permission to initiate and fail.

We actually solved the three major problems at the end of the meeting. The group responded and came to a conclusion—a plan for a solution.

The point is that in order to solve conflict, you need to get emotionally involved and then work on a solution. The keys are listening and getting people to share emotion. If these problems hadn't been solved, this huge 8,000-person communication company would have gone bankrupt in a year.

## THE COMMUNICATION PROCESS

In the process of communication, seek first to understand what your protégé is saying. This is done in three steps. First, listen to what he is saying. Do not merely hear him, but hone in on exactly what he is trying to communicate. Next, ask questions to clarify until you are sure that your "picture" matches his. Finally, empathize with the person by expressing understanding, similar experiences, or genuine emotion over the things he has shared.

In communicating with your mentoree, seek to be understood properly. Encourage your protégé to use the same methods to understand exactly what you are communicating. Or you can "ask" the questions for him!

Good communication does not result in confusion or misunderstandings. It is often true that we say something, we understand it, and we think it is clear, but the other person just doesn't understand what we are saying. Someone has said that the natural result of communication is confusion. This can be overcome if you are willing to put some effort into the process of communication.

> Good communication does **not** result in confusion or misunderstandings.

The need to know the person to whom you are communicating is vital if you really want to communicate effectively. This cannot be emphasized enough. Does she have a tendency to forget important things? Does she take everything you say literally? This knowledge will equip you to accommodate her and still allow communication to take place.

### WATCH YOUR TONGUE

The tongue, though small, has a large and important role. James 3:5–6 says, "The tongue is a small part of the body, but it makes great boasts. Consider what a great forest is set on fire by a small spark. The tongue also is a fire." You can do more harm with an inappropriately stated word than you would ever imagine. Friendships have been destroyed by an inappropriate sentence or a loss of temper. Mentoring relationships have been discounted through slander and ridicule.

Although many animals have fancier tongues than man, man's tongue alone can form words. And these words can make or break a man. Sir Walter Raleigh once stated, "It is observed in the course of worldly things that man's fortunes are oftener made by their tongues [than] by their virtues, and more men's fortunes overthrown thereby than by vices." The same can be said with the mentoring process.

Just as a word improperly said can be destructive, a word fitly spoken can give new delights, make a plain person into a beautiful person, heal bruises, soothe agitated tempers, give hope to despondent souls, and point the way to God. Scripture clearly defines for us the appropriate use of the tongue. Ephesians 4:25-32 says:

> Therefore each of you must put off falsehood and speak truthfully to his neighbor, for we are all members of one body. "In your anger do not sin": Do not let the sun go down while you are still angry, and do not give the devil a foothold. He who has been stealing must steal no longer, but must

work, doing something useful with his own hands, that he may have something to share with those in need.

Do not let any unwholesome talk come out of your mouths, but only what is helpful for building others up according to their needs, that it may benefit those who listen. And do not grieve the Holy Spirit of God, with whom you were sealed for the day of redemption. Get rid of all bitterness, rage and anger, brawling and slander, along with every form of malice. Be kind and compassionate to one another, forgiving each other, just as in Christ God forgave you.

There are three points from this passage which relate to our communication. First, our words are to be true. Paul says in verse 25, "Put off falsehood and speak truthfully." Today is a day of tremendous duplicity and falsehood. So often we get caught in subtle lies or even overt ones. Remember the following in order to put off falsehood and speak truthfully:

1. Avoid half-truths. Don't just tell the part of the story that makes you look good.

2. Distinguish between fact and opinion. Don't state something as reality when it is simply your opinion. Use the phrase "I think" or "In my opinion."

3. Be careful about absolute statements. For example, "You never tell me what you are thinking" or "I always have to repeat myself" are not true statements. They are exaggerations and, in essence, are lies.

4. Be honest and truthful about yourself. Admit when you are wrong or when you can't do something.

5. Be careful of "white lies." A lie is never acceptable.

The second point to consider about the appropriate use of the tongue is that we ought to be kind. Ephesians 4:31–32 says, "Get rid of all bitterness, rage and anger, brawling and slander, along with every form of malice. Be kind and compassionate to one another, forgiving each other, just as in Christ God forgave you." We are never to say unkind words. Neither are we to send unkind messages non-verbally.

The third point to consider from this passage is that we are to say only things which are necessary. In verse 29, we read, "Do not let any unwholesome talk come out of your mouths, but only what is helpful for building others up according to their needs, that it may benefit those who listen." Paul is saying that we are not to speak unless it will build up someone or meet a need. A New England proverb states "Don't talk unless you can improve the silence."

> "Don't talk unless you can improve the silence."

The point is clear: We should speak when we are encouraging or uplifting our mentorees; we should never be cruel; and we should always be truthful.

## LISTENING

Effective communication does not involve talking as much as it involves listening. Remember the words of Polonius in Hamlet, "Give every man thine ear, but few thy voice." You will never understand your protégé's perspective unless you truly listen to him. Without understanding, communication has not taken place.

We are to be "quick to hear and slow to speak" (James 1:19). This is radically different from how most of us behave. We tend to want to "fix things" before we have fully comprehended what we are hearing. Communication cannot be rushed and must be based on careful listening.

Careful listening is never done unintentionally. This is harder for some people, but it is a *learned skill* for everyone. With practice, you can develop a "talent" for listening that will serve you well in the mentoring process.

## PUT THE SPEAKER AT EASE

Establish and maintain an open and receptive atmosphere in the discussion. Don't make the person feel that you are ready to jump on every word spoken. Sometimes our "fix-it" mindset hurts this process. Though you need to build into people, confront them appropriately, and be forthright, you must also help people to open up. This will happen as they know you authentically care for them. Remember, "People do not care how much you know until they know how much you care."

Praying for your mentoree while you are in conversation can enable you to keep the right perspective. Ask God for wisdom to assertively understand and meet needs in your protégé's life. Ask God to give you perception and clarity as you seek to comprehend what you are hearing.

> Ask God for **wisdom** to assertively understand and meet **needs** in your protégé's life.

Allow your mentoree to see that you are a good listener. Respond to questions directly and fully. Ask meaningful questions that show you are listening such as, "Could you explain what you mean by the word fear?" If your mentoree feels at ease, the communication process will be simplified.

## DON'T AVOID CONTROVERSY

Avoiding controversy is impossible if you are in relationship with others. Scripture demands that Christian men and women maintain a spirit of unity. Ephesians 4:3 says, "Make every effort to keep the unity of the Spirit through the bond of peace." But this does not mean that we must agree on everything. Paul and Barnabas sharply disagreed about bringing John Mark along on a visit to the young Christian churches in Acts 15.36–41 (and they were in a mentoring-type relationship!).

We are bound to disagree, even with those that we mentor. We simply need to disagree in a loving and firm way. Therefore, don't try to dodge disagreement or controversy. Simply handle it appropriately. That is, be respectful, listen to the other person, and, if necessary, agree to disagree.

The tendency is to "stuff it" (i.e. bury your feelings or views) or "strike out" (i.e. get upset, yell, demand, or argue). Both of these are inappropriate. The key is to "speak the truth in love" (Ephesians 4:15). Nothing is lost by being truthful and loving at all times.

### REMOVE DISTRACTIONS

Mentoring should be an intentional time that is reserved for the specific protégé and nothing else. Since appointments are often brief, and there is usually much to cover, take care to remove distractions from your meeting. Don't doodle on your papers or answer your cell phone if at all possible. Concentrate on the person in front of you and on the things that she is saying.

I (Ron) am impressed by former U.S. Senator Bill Armstrong. Whenever I have met with this incredibly busy man, he has given me his total attention and made me feel very important. I've noticed that he does this with everyone. This is a perfect example of artful communication.

Since you have agreed to invest in the life of your mentoree, allow him to have your full and undivided attention throughout your time together. This does not mean that you must pretend that you have nothing else to do and nowhere else to be. This means that you let him know non-verbally that he is so worthwhile to you that you are willing to shut off the world while you talk with him.

### EMPATHIZE WITH THE PERSON

During the communication process, try to put yourself in the other person's shoes. This means attempting to see the topic or problem from your mentoree's perspective. This is a very difficult thing to do, but it must be done if there is to be effective communication.

You can use phrases such as "I understand," "That must be very painful," or "I can see why you are so excited." These show your mentoree that you are listening and that you care about what she is saying. You might also find that striving to show empathy will actually make you more empathetic.

## BE PATIENT

Communication doesn't happen quickly or without much effort; it takes time. Don't get frustrated and upset, but give yourself plenty of time to listen without interruption. Then ask penetrating questions so that you arrive at a mutual understanding. Don't allow yourself to jump to conclusions. Patiently seek to understand what the other person means by what he says.

It can be frustrating to hear the same things over and over. Often people need to discuss the same topics and rehash the same predicaments many times.

> Often, you can **help** people reach a conclusion **simply** by listening and asking **intelligent** questions.

It is worth it to be patient during this process since a listening ear is often the "solution" to the felt need of talking over the subject. Often, you can help people reach a conclusion simply by listening and asking intelligent questions.

## ASK QUESTIONS

Asking questions will encourage your protégé and show her that you are listening. Furthermore, the responses will help you understand her point of view. You might ask a question such as, "Could you clarify that last point?" or "What do you mean by that?" or "How does that make you feel?"

Ted's mentoree, Michael D. Vessey, shares the following about Ted's methods of communicating, "Ted does not mentor to create people in his own image. His goal is to help his charge discover God's plan for his life. Ted then helps draw out how that plan works in real life.

"Ted could compete with Socrates when it comes to asking questions. This is his main method of teaching. He is a master at pinpointing just the question that needs to be asked. He has asked me thousands of questions about my life, my relationships with other people, my relationship with God, my work, my clients, my vision for my future, and most importantly, about my wife and kids.

"For every answer given, Ted asks another question. His purpose is to make me think about why I am doing what I am doing. There is never a time that I don't come away from lunch with Ted feeling as if I need to re-evaluate everything I am about."

The communication between you and your mentoree can have the same positive impact. Try to implement question asking, patience, empathy, honesty, and intent-listening—you'll see your communication grow more purposeful and productive. You can and do communicate thousands of messages every day. Make sure that the messages you send to your mentoree are the ones that you intend for her to hear. And, when listening, pay close attention, and you may discover that there is much that you have never "heard" before!

The key to any relationship is healthy communication. Especially in your mentoring relationships, put effort into making the communication as strong as possible in order to impact your protégé's life as much as possible.

OTHER LEADERS SAY . . .

*"This chapter is a great example of the idea that sometimes we don't need new truths so much as we need to be reminded of the old truths we already know. There's nothing magical or radical about the ideas in this chapter—listen to others, watch your tongue, tell the truth, be kind, be patient—but if we can teach ourselves to put these ideas into practice on a regular basis the results will be truly amazing.*

*"One way to do this is to examine your communication with your mentoree after each session with him. What went well? What could have gone better? Did you interrupt when you should have listened? Do you feel that true understanding was achieved? Because we all communicate all of the time, we often just take it for granted. But if you consciously make an effort to evaluate and improve your contributions to the communication process you'll find that your communication skills—and your personal relationships—take a turn for the better."*

—DOUG TROUTEN is director of the Evangelical Press Association. He teaches journalism at Northwestern College in St. Paul, Minnesota.

*"Drs. Engstrom and Jensen's chapter on communication shows just how 'a word fitly spoken can give new delights, make a plain person into a beautiful person, heal bruises, soothe agitated tempers, give hope to despondent souls, and point the way to God.' Those we mentor along life's unchartable road need such practical and purposeful help. So do we. Learning to listen and to say what needs to be said when it needs to be said are skills this chapter can help every reader acquire—skills that will infuse our mentoring with meaning."*

—DR. MARTY TRAMMELL chairs the English/Communication program at Corban College (formerly Western Baptist College). For the past twenty years, he and his wife, Linda, have mentored engaged couples at the college and teens and families at Valley Baptist of Perrydale, Oregon.

*"I remember communications classes at the university and in seminary: how to prepare speeches, how to communicate effectively on radio and television, how to write persuasively, how to present effective, life-changing sermons. But I don't remember a class teaching what I've learned to be a vital aspect of communication: listening.*

*"As professional communicators, we're pretty good at talking and writing. However, I've been reminded on a number of occasions that I need to learn to be a better listener. My assistant reminded me of that one day as I fingered through a stack of papers on my desk while she was trying to talk to me. A friend on the phone hearing my computer keys in the background asked if I was working on email. Busted!!*

*"If we're to improve in our communication skills, we must seek to understand before we can be understood. Actively listening and asking thought-provoking questions can do more to ensure that the picture we have in our minds matches the picture in the mind of our listener.*

*"As a Type A and a high I (Meyers-Briggs), it's a skill I'm still trying to master. As Proverbs 15:28 says, 'The godly think before speaking.' And Proverbs 17:27: 'A truly wise person uses few words; a person with understanding is even-tempered.'"*

—WAYNE PEDERSON is manager of WMBI AM-FM in Chicago, flagship station for the Moody Broadcasting Network. He's worked in leadership positions at Northwestern College Radio, National Religious Broadcasters, Mission America, and Bethel University.

*"What is mentoring without communication? Nonexistent! And effective communication is all about the right use of our ears and our tongues. This chapter on communication is a must for anyone interested in mentoring God's way. First we use our ears liberally and then our tongues with great restraint. In my view of leadership, 'listen' is the most important word in a leader's vocabulary. Listening is a key ingredient for good communication, and leadership is all about communicating well. I cannot emphasize enough how crucial communication is to getting things done through people.*

*"In this thoughtful process of communication outlined by Engstrom and Jenson in this chapter, they clearly lay out the importance of listening for communication—as well as a strategy for listening effectively. I really appreciate*

*their treatment of the counterbalance to listening: the op-*
*posite task—speaking with our tongues. I like their careful*
*handling of how dangerous this tiny weapon is for good*
*and harm. God gave us our two ears to listen well and*
*our one tongue to communicate positively. As James said*
*so well, we are to be 'quick to hear and slow to speak'*
*(James 1:19)."*

—DR. HANS FINZEL *is the president of CBInternational*
*in Littleton, Colorado, and is the best-selling author of*
The Top Ten Mistakes Leaders Make.

*"Communicating seems so simple. But if something we*
*say can be misunderstood, it probably will be. Anyone*
*who's been in leadership more than an hour and a half*
*has no doubt realized that what people hear us say is not*
*what we thought we said. They read (and misread) our*
*words, gestures, facial expressions, and tone of voice.*

*"That's why the principles that Ted and Ron identify in*
*this chapter are so important. They minimize the risk of*
*misunderstanding. And their principles do something*
*more—they put the emphasis where it belongs for a*
*mentor: on clarifying the thoughts of the mentoree. As*
*an editor, my job is to help writers clarify what they're*
*thinking, so they can write articles that communicate.*
*Likewise, mentors don't succeed by talking, even when*
*their talking drips with jewels of wisdom. Instead, by lis-*
*tening and asking good questions mentors bring out the*
*best thoughts of their mentorees.*

*"One young man was describing two professors who were*
*serving as his mentors. 'When I listen to Professor Abbot,*
*I go away impressed with his brilliance, but when I talk*

*with Professor Parsons, I go away thinking I've got some-*
*thing significant to offer.'*

*Guess which professor was the better communicator? Not*
*the brilliant talker, but the one who asked the right ques-*
*tions and listened well."*

—MARSHALL SHELLEY *is a vice president of*
*Christianity Today International and editor of*
*Leadership, a journal for church leaders.*

## HOW ABOUT YOU?

Determine your level of proficiency in the area of communication from the chart below. 1 is the lowest, 10 is the highest with 5 as average.

## COMMUNICATION

| 1 | 1.5 | 2 | 2.5 | 3 | 3.5 | 4 | 4.5 | 5 | 5.5 | 6 | 6.5 | 7 | 7.5 | 8 | 8.5 | 9 | 9.5 | 10 |
|---|-----|---|-----|---|-----|---|-----|---|-----|---|-----|---|-----|---|-----|---|-----|----|

What do you need to do in order to improve half of a point this week in your mentoring relationships?

*"An honest man's the noblest work of God."*
—ALEXANDER POPE

*"God will continue to use your honesty and vulnerability about your experiences to strengthen the faith of others who are suffering and feeling alone."*
—JAMES DOBSON

# HONESTY

F or us to experience personal progress means that people notice that we are not the same person that we were yesterday. We do not need to hide the fact that we are not perfect. As we gain the ability to be honest before people, we are on the way toward healthy openness and growth. Honesty involves realizing that you are not perfect and learning how to share your feelings constructively.

Scripture clearly states that our lives are an open book to God. Hebrews 4:12–13 says, "For the word of God is living and active. Sharper than any double-edged sword, it penetrates even to dividing soul and spirit, joints and marrow; it judges the thoughts and attitudes of the heart. Nothing in all creation is hidden from God's sight. Everything is uncovered and laid bare before the eyes of him to whom we must give account."

What does it mean that the Word of God "penetrates"? It means that God is interested in the penetration of our facade, our mask. God wants to touch the innermost part of our hearts. He wants to sift out and analyze our thoughts and intentions, what we are thinking about, reflecting upon, and feeling. We are, in effect, absolutely bare before him, so nothing is hidden from him. Yet he wants us, and waits for us, to ask him to point out areas in our lives that need to be brought into conformity to his will. In Psalm 139:23-24, David writes, "Search me, O God, and know my heart; test me and know my anxious thoughts. See if there is any offensive way in me, and lead me in the way everlasting." David was crying out to God to point out in him anything that would prevent an intimate relationship with the Father.

> [God] wants us, and waits for us, to ask him to point out areas in our lives that need to be brought into conformity to his will.

Not only is God interested in our being open with him, he is also interested in our being open with other people. Scripture offers many illustrations and statements about our need for honesty and vulnerability with one another. Throughout his writings and especially in the book of 2 Corinthians, for instance, Paul writes very freely about some of the struggles he has had. He says at one point that, "We do not want you to be uninformed, brothers, about the hardships we suffered in the province of Asia. We were under great pressure, far beyond our ability to endure, so that we despaired even of life" (2 Corinthians 1:8). Paul was extremely open and honest about the struggles and difficulties that he had.

It is important to define what transparency is *not*. It is not unloading all the dirt in your life. Transparency is also not an excuse to share all your emotional problems or to live with your emotions on your sleeve. We are not to think that openness or vulnerability means sharing negative thoughts and feelings in the name of honesty. It is still honest and yet not damaging to share with your mentoree just what she needs to know, and no more.

A good example of such openness can be found in the New Testament. Paul writes the following to the people of Corinth in 2 Corinthians 4:7–12, 16–18:

> But we have this treasure in jars of clay to show that this all-surpassing power is from God and not from us. We are hard pressed on every side, but not crushed; perplexed, but not abandoned; struck down, but not destroyed. We always carry around in our body the death of Jesus, so that the life of Jesus may also be revealed in our body. For we who are alive are always being given over to death for Jesus' sake, so that his life may be revealed in our mortal body. So then, death is at work in us, but life is at work in you.

> Therefore we do not lose heart. Though outwardly we are wasting away, yet inwardly we are being renewed day by day. For our light and momentary troubles are achieving for us an eternal glory that far outweighs them all. So we fix our eyes not on what is seen, but on what is unseen. For what is seen is temporary, but what is unseen is eternal.

Paul experienced intense pressure and pain, and he freely communicated that pain to his brothers and sisters in Christ in Corinth. He also communicated that in the midst of the difficulty, he emerged with a jubilant, victorious, positive statement about how God was giving him the ultimate victory.

In 2 Corinthians 12:7-10, the apostle Paul tells the Corinthians that he has received a "thorn in my flesh" to keep him from becoming conceited about his abilities and gifts. Paul doesn't tell them all of the "dirty" details, but he also does not act prideful and gloss over his weaknesses. He tells them plainly that he is not perfect and has to rely on Christ's strength in everything that he does. This is a good example of healthy honesty which allows others to see weaknesses but does not revel in them.

> Healthy honesty . . . allows others to see weaknesses but does not revel in them.

There are two specific things that you can do in order to demonstrate and develop the kind of openness that Paul models. First, realize that you are not yet perfect (and won't be until heaven). With this acknowledgment, you can start to deal with the normal fear of being open. Second, learn how to share your feelings in order to be open and honest with those around you, especially your mentoree.

### REALIZE YOU ARE NOT PERFECT

Mentors do not have to pretend to be perfect; they will be most effective when they can share their own struggles, history, and mistakes. Allow your protégé to watch the process of Christ perfecting you in him. If you pretend to have it all together, you will frustrate and discourage your mentoree. He will know himself well enough to realize that perfection is unattainable in this life. If you appear perfect, you will be discounted. Remember, he already knows that there is no such thing as a perfect person!

Instead, welcome your mentoree into your life so that he may have a look around. There is so much that he can learn from your mistakes and struggles. For example, he can watch you deal with disappointment and learn how to deal effectively with his own. Your acknowledgment and treatment of sin will shape his view and handling of it.

> Your acknowledgment and treatment of sin will shape your mentoree's view and handling of it.

Since we learn best with visuals and personal experience, not empty words of "you should" or "you ought to," open your mentoree's vision to include your mistakes and experiences (whether positive or negative). Allow her to learn vicariously through you and so pass on what you have learned and the advancements that you have made.

There is no more powerful way to be honest with your mentoree than to let them into your life in a literal sense. My (Ron) wife, Mary, and I took a trip many years ago with a couple we mentored, Alan and Theda Hlavka. I include Alan's words to demonstrate living in front of, and for, your protégé. Alan says, "Ron and Mary invited us to participate in one of the most unique and influential discipleship experiences of our lives. Ron was going to conduct a research project in the area of discipleship for his doctorate by traveling to thirty-eight states and 175 ministries across the nation over a period of seven months. Theda and I were asked to travel with them in a twenty-foot motor home. We lived together, day in and day out, for seven months!

"Everyone told us we were crazy to attempt such an endeavor. 'Living in those tight quarters with little or no break from each other will prove disastrous!' we were told. What was predicted by many to be a relationally foolish move on all our parts, ended up being what Theda and I consider to be the single greatest mentoring experience of our lives. We didn't just hear about what it meant to see the life of Jesus in someone's life, we experienced it morning through night every day. Ron mentored us all (he had also led his wife Mary to Christ in the early days of their friendship). Quite frankly, Theda and I were anxious to see if the effervescent joy that we had witnessed at a distance was a reality in the daily stuff of life. We were *not* disappointed!

"Did Ron live perfectly during those seven months? No. But when he did quench the Spirit through a word or deed, he quickly repented, took responsibility, sought forgiveness, and returned to the joy of an intimate walk with him. In was remarkable. It was real. It was life marking. As the trip progressed, my hunger for ministry intensified. I had a desire to effectively impact students because of what I saw in Ron's life."

Most people don't have such opportunities for around the clock mentorship. But you can do this on a smaller scale. If it is appropriate to your mentoring relationship, invite your mentoree to your home where she can watch you interact with your spouse and children. Invite her to observe your life in action in order to gain a rounder view.

Realizing that you are in process and are not perfect should be very freeing. Although there are guidelines to healthy honesty which we discuss below, being honest with your mentoree will swing wide the gates of effective communication and lasting life change.

**Being honest with your mentoree will swing wide the gates of effective communication and lasting life change.**

## LEARN HOW TO SHARE YOUR FEELINGS

The second step in becoming open with your mentoree is learning to share your feelings and listen carefully to his feelings. Listening to your mentoree's feelings and emotions involves seeking to understand them. Yet, whether you understand the why or not, it is vital to accept what he feels without disagreeing or getting angry.

Make your questions honest inquiries for information. If you ask with the right motives and communicate care for your protégé, then you will find it is easier for both of you to honestly share your feelings.

Avoid statements beginning with "you." These statements usually come across as a personal attack. Instead, phrase sentences in this way: "I feel like you don't value our time together when you show up late for our meetings." This will allow communication to take place. Statements such as "You are lazy and disrespectful" always halt constructive, helpful conversation.

Do not insult, criticize, or yell. This may seem obvious, but it is a good reminder to watch your tone of voice, use of "jokes" (i.e. harsh comments disguised as jokes), and how you share your personal opinions. What may be normal or inoffensive to you can be quite damaging and hurtful to another. If you are in doubt, ask a trusted friend for her opinion. Certainly, raising your voice or using profane or offensive language is never in order.

State clearly how you feel, but do it in love with the desire to build up the other person, not tear him down. There is much to be said for a strong word that is spoken in love. Proverbs 24:26 says, "An honest answer is like a kiss on the lips."

Do not bring up past experiences that have created bad feelings. If you desire to have a mentoring relationship built on honesty, it will require that you allow your protégé to be honest by not "punishing" him for past honesty. For example, if your mentoree shared three months ago that he was feeling unsuccessful at work because of a missed deadline, there is no reason to continue to refer to that disappointment. Let the past shared honesty be separate from the present.

If you have a conflict with your mentoree, be sure to solve it. Moreover, don't neglect to delve in to the original reasons for the problem. Analyzing the situation and what caused it to occur will eliminate many future conflicts. It will also give both of you understanding of the other's life and way of thinking and processing.

## HEALTHY HONESTY

Perhaps you've experienced cruel honesty in which words were spoken that, while quite possibly true, were cutting or humiliating. Honesty requires sensitivity to timing, character, and level of relationship. In the mentoring relationship, there is often a platform to speak honestly into your mentoree's life since the relationship is built on the desire for growth and change. However, this cannot be assumed and should not be abused. Take care to explore the level of honesty that is appropriate for your particular relationship.

Above all, it is vital for people to be honest with God and honest with themselves. Honesty with yourself involves introspection and critical thinking. It may also include the opinion of a trusted friend, relative, or mentor. An honest look at your life may cause you to think, "I do well in new situations and with people I have never met before" or "I need assistance in keeping my schedule realistic." These kinds of statements are not self-bashing or ego-boosting. They are an honest look at what you excel and struggle at. More than that, the purpose of such statements is to set goals, evaluate needs, and act accordingly.

Honesty with God cannot be overemphasized. The Scriptures have numerous examples of people who were honest with God in their fears, sins, triumphs, and grief. He desires honesty (and reverence). If you do not have a relationship with him, it is never too late to start. Even if you already do, begin to be honest with him by confessing your sins, sharing your fears, and thanking him for his goodness to you. Psalm 139:3-4 says, "You are familiar with all my ways. Before a word is on my tongue you know it completely, O LORD." It's safe to bring our honest reflections, questions, and doubts to him. After all, he already knows them and he still wants to have a relationship with us!

On the human level, complete honesty is appropriate in selected relationships and with particular people.

For husbands and wives, complete honesty is a key to an intimate marriage. Between very close friends, it is often acceptable. However, in the mentoring relationship, it usually is not.

> On the human level, **complete** honesty is appropriate in **selected** relationships and with **particular** people.

In most relationships, guarded honesty is the rule. Healthy honesty is not unloading every detail of your life and sharing negative thoughts and feelings. It is attention to what you share and what you don't share *for the sake of everyone involved.* Unnecessary honesty (that which is reserved for your relationships with God and your most intimate friends) puts a burden on you and your mentoree that will strain the mentoring process.

Choose to share details and stories that will build up your mentoree, even if they cast you in a negative light. Be especially careful to not "tell on" others who are not able to tell their side of the story or defend themselves. While it may be acceptable to share negative stories about your own errors or unfortunate circumstances, it is generally not acceptable to share other people's "dirt."

Openness within the mentoring relationship lets your protégé see the real you, the person that makes mistakes and learns from them. Without honesty, your relationship will have much difficulty in achieving depth and strength.

Bobb Biehl shares the following wisdom, "*Be open and transparent.* One of the things that my wife, Cheryl, has often told me is this: 'Your associate team only hears about your successes. Let them hear also about your failures.' I have to watch very carefully that I tell my associate team not only when I have won, and when the client has said yes, and when I have given counsel that works, but also when I have failed to win a client, and/or when a bit of advice to a client has not worked.

"Every mentor has struggles that the protégé never sees. The protégé might say with some hesitation, 'My mentor can do this, but I don't know if I'll ever make it because I have problems with discipline (or doubt, or self-worth, or fatigue, etc.).'

"Be humble enough to share with a protégé, not your dirty laundry, not your skeletons in the closet from thirty years ago, but your struggles today, along with the things you are trying to teach."

Your openness will give your mentoree the chance to view your decisions, responses, failures, and successes in order to glean wisdom for his own life. However, be careful to keep your "honesty" both healthy and appropriate to the relationship. Too many details and unnecessary information may actually damage your success as a mentor. It is not that mentors with checkered pasts should not share what they have learned. Nor is it that mentors with struggles and problems (that is, all mentors!) should pretend that they don't have issues for the sake of the protégé. Instead, it is that mentors should use caution and wisdom as they seek to share their heart and life, without overstepping the bounds of healthy honesty.

OTHER LEADERS SAY . . .

*"I especially appreciated the distinctions between guard-ed, complete, unnecessary, and healthy honesty. My first*

*mentor, Pastor Nick Harris, exemplified healthy honesty. So many people will only offer you what you want to hear or more than you need to hear. My mentor and pastor had the wisdom to carefully and honestly reveal his personal weaknesses to help me overcome mine. His transparent vulnerability allowed me to see firsthand how to find strength and security in Christ in the middle of haunting personal doubts and insecurities. Without a doubt, his healthy honesty was the most valuable quality in our mentoring relationship. Getting vulnerable, transparent and real seems risky. It is a risk that is worth the reward."*

—PASTOR CRAIG GROESCHEL is founding and senior pastor of Life Church (www.lifechurch.tv), one of the largest and fastest-growing churches in America.

*"Honesty and integrity are cherished, though often neglected character qualities. Mark Twain retorted, 'Always do right. It will gratify some people and astonish the rest.' Others have said that character is what a person does if they knew they would never be found out. Perhaps the later is more of what we saw in such places as Enron, Adelphia, Global Crossing, Worldcom, and the rest. Sadly, it seems that many in leadership these days are not looking . . . or if they are, not too carefully. We seem to have focused on education, technological skills, degrees, travel experience, and the other 'surface' qualities so much that we have too often forgotten the core issues that are what truly makes the difference.*

*"Notice God's evaluation of leadership, though, when he described one of the greatest leaders of all time, King Da-*

*vid.* *'And David shepherded them with integrity of heart; with skillful hands he led them' (Psalm 78:72). Notice the order—not competency first and then integrity, but character first, and then competency! Character is the bedrock from which competency can best operate. It is why David himself said, 'Surely you desire truth in the inner parts . . .' (Psalm 51:6). While everyone else looks on external accomplishments, the Ultimate Judge is looking far deeper . . . at what you and I are really in the depths of our hearts. That's the mark of a true leader!"*

—DR. ROBERT E. "BOB" RECCORD became the first president of NAMB in 1997. NAMB fields approximately 5,200 missionaries across North America. He received his master of divinity and doctor of ministry degrees from Southwestern Baptist Theological Seminary in Fort Worth, Texas. He has been a speaker for Promise Keepers and Ken Blanchard's "Lead Like Jesus" Celebrations.

*"I love the challenging statement in this chapter: 'Welcome your mentoree into your life so that he may have a look around. There is so much that he can learn from your mistakes and struggles.' For years I wanted to run and hide from my mistakes, struggles, and weaknesses. I still do, but my good friend Karl constantly prays that I will know, share, and minister out of my weakness. Karl knows about weakness. Confined to a wheelchair, requiring 24-hour a day nursing care, Karl constantly calls me to live and breathe that very counter-cultural theme of Gospel spirituality: God shines through our weaknesses.*

*"As the authors so clearly declare, if we don't share the specific stories of our failures and weaknesses—at the*

*right time and in the right spirit—our mentorees may never face their own weaknesses. But as we share our struggles, they watch—up close and personal—the glory of God flowing into and gushing out of an ordinary cracked vessel. I can't think of a more beautiful gift to give another human being."*

—MATHEW WOODLEY, a Minnesota native, serves as the senior pastor at the The Three Village Church on Long Island, New York. A frequent contributor to *Discipleship Journal* and *Leadership*, Matt just finished his first book, *Holy Fools*, to be released in 2006 by NavPress.

*"Being honest and vulnerable is the key to bonding with your mentoree. Passing on knowledge feeds the mind but transparency pours hope into the heart. While advocating honesty, the author wisely gives boundaries: consider the impact of your words and share only what builds up. Dumping details of intimate sins or negative opinions about others is honesty without wisdom. Sharing Christ's work in your life of conviction, forgiveness, and restoration inspires and encourages your mentoree to press on, together with you, towards Christ-likeness."*

—POPPY SMITH, a former Bible Study Fellowship lecturer, passionately encourages women to hunger for a deeper walk with Jesus Christ through her speaking, writing, and counseling ministry (www.poppysmith.com).

## HOW ABOUT YOU?

Determine your level of proficiency in the area of

honesty from the chart below. 1 is the lowest, 10 is the highest with 5 as average.

HONESTY

| 1 | 1.5 | 2 | 2.5 | 3 | 3.5 | 4 | 4.5 | 5 | 5.5 | 6 | 6.5 | 7 | 7.5 | 8 | 8.5 | 9 | 9.5 | 10 |
|---|-----|---|-----|---|-----|---|-----|---|-----|---|-----|---|-----|---|-----|---|-----|----|

What do you need to do in order to improve half of a point this week in your mentoring relationships?

*"Take that gift God has entrusted to you;
and use it in the service of Christ and your fellow
men. He will make it glow and shine like
the very stars of heaven."*
—JOHN BONNELL

*"Every person I have known who has been truly happy
has learned how to serve others."*
—ALBERT SCHWEITZER

# Chapter 7
# SERVANTHOOD

**J**esus Christ turned the disciples' thinking upside down one night with a symbolic act of love. They must have wondered, "Why is the Messiah washing dirty feet before the Passover Feast? If this man is truly the Son of God, why is he rinsing the dust off of the weary feet of his followers?" Peter was so perplexed that he actually challenged his Master, "Are you going to wash my feet? . . . No, you shall never wash my feet."

Jesus finished washing their feet and answered the questions that hung in the air. "Now that I, your Lord and Teacher, have washed your feet, you also should wash one another's feet. I have set you an example that you should do as I have done for you. . . . Now that you know these things, you will be blessed if you do them" (see John 13:1–17). If the Master considered foot washing—generally a servant's duty—to be his rightful task, perhaps we should take a look at his call for us to serve as he did.

Jesus was the ideal mentor and leader. Although he had the right to exert authority over his protégés (that is, his disciples), he continually served them and allowed them to be a part of his work. From his life and work, we can glean many principles for mentoring. Specifically, Jesus was humble, willing to make sacrifices, and he was a servant leader.

First Thessalonians 2:9 allows us to draw many conclusions about servanthood. Paul says, "Surely you remember, brothers, our toil and hardship; we worked night and day in order not to be a burden to anyone while we preached the gospel of God to you." In this passage, Paul clearly states that he and his co-workers were living a certain kind of lifestyle. They were not living as weak and pathetic individuals, lacking will and purpose. They were real men, choosing to live a life of service to others in the name of their powerful and risen Lord Jesus Christ. These men modeled servanthood done with a humble attitude.

Humility is not inferiority. Romans 12:3 tells us that we are not to think more highly of ourselves than we ought to. This does not imply that we are to have an inferior view of ourselves, but a healthy one. We know that we are people of great worth, according to Scripture. No one is inferior, and to view yourself as such is not true humility.

> Humility . . . does **not imply** that we are to have an inferior view of ourselves, but a **healthy** one.

Humility is not an underestimation of our abilities. Describing himself, Paul writes, "Actually I should have been commended by you, for in no respect was I inferior to the most eminent apostles, even though I am a nobody" (2 Corinthians 12:11). Paul has a good sense of his own abilities. In 1 Corinthians 12 and in Ephesians 4, we read that God has given each one of us unique gifts and abilities. These gifts and abilities are absolutely necessary to building up the body of Christ. It takes each part of the body working correctly within its purpose in order for the body to function as a whole.

Therefore, you cannot underestimate your abilities, background, contacts, position, or any other asset no matter how trivial they may seem. Since they are given by God, they must be handled with great respect and admiration. You must be a good steward of these gifts as you strive to glorify God. Mentoring is a perfect example. If you have the gift of encouragement, leadership, or hospitality, etc., then you can use it to serve your mentoree.

Humility is not self-hatred. Understanding that we are sinful does not mean we need to hate ourselves. Psalm 139 tells of God's wonderful work in making our physical form and our non-physical substance (including our personalities). We cannot rightfully hate that which God fashioned while we were still in our mothers' wombs.

Humility is not passivity. Again, we think of the example of Jesus Christ, who was the most vibrant manifestation of humility in all of Scripture. He was the same one who overturned the tables of the moneychangers and the benches of those selling doves and chased them out of the house of God (Matthew 21:12–13). He was bold, aggressive, and righteously angry at those who upset the things of God.

> Humility means **staying** broken and yielded to God on the one hand and **resting** in the power of God to **work** through us on the other hand.

However, Jesus wasn't on a power trip. Humility means staying broken and yielded to God on the one hand and resting in the power of God to work through us on the other hand. In mentoring, humility requires that we stay yielded to the Lord and constantly maintain brokenness. God wants you to be constantly yielded to him so that you can do his will, not your own. That is the very heart of humility—staying yielded to God.

What does such a life of brokenness look like? It means spending time daily with God because you know you need his power and insight. It means not demanding your own way even if you are right. It means leaning into God throughout the day—turning to him for clarity, wisdom, sensitivity, and empowerment. It means maintaining a sweet, kind, gentle, open, tender spirit before God and man. It means being teachable. If you can maintain brokenness by God's grace, then you will have the foundation of usability before God in your mentoring endeavors.

If you can maintain **brokenness** by God's grace, then you will have the **foundation** of usability before God in your **mentoring** endeavors.

Humility believes that God will work through you and your gifts. Romans 12:3 says that we are not to think more highly of ourselves than we ought to. Then Paul goes on to say that we should exercise the various gifts each one of us has been given (Romans 12:6). A truly humble person is one who knows his strengths and his weaknesses, who appreciates both, and who learns how to handle both. We need to work on our weaknesses. We also need to focus on our strengths. Mostly, we need to be aware of both and learn how to live in light of our strengths and weaknesses.

Humility is recognizing our need of God, realistically evaluating our capacities, and being willing to serve. Based on this attitude of humility, biblical servanthood manifests a life of sacrificial giving.

## SACRIFICIAL GIVING

A true Christian does not shy away from the work of giving himself to other people, including his mentoree. You cannot give to others in an impersonal, at-arm's-length manner. Giving involves personal time and effort. It often means that your schedule and your approach may need to be adapted to fit your protégé's needs. Giving involves commitment.

> A true **Christian** does not shy away from the work of **giving** himself to other people, **including** his mentoree.

Being a servant involves sacrificial giving. In 1 Thessalonians 2:9, Paul says that he, Timothy, and Silas "worked night and day." These men were living sacrificially as they gave of themselves. The concept of sacrificially giving ourselves to others is seen throughout Scripture. Galatians 5:13 says, "You, my brothers, were called to be free. But do not use your freedom to indulge the sinful nature; rather, serve one another in love."

Hebrews 10:24 says, "And let us consider how we may spur one another on toward love and good deeds." Likewise, Romans 12:10-13 instructs us, "Be devoted to one another in brotherly love. Honor one another above yourselves. Never be lacking in zeal, but keep your spiritual fervor, serving the Lord. Be joyful in hope, patient in affliction, faithful in prayer. Share with God's people who are in need. Practice hospitality."

At the heart of these passages is an attitude of sacrificial giving of one's life, one's time, one's gifts, and one's finances. The classic passage on the giving of finances is 2 Corinthians 8:1-5. However, this passage has a great deal to do with giving in general.

> And now, brothers, we want you to know about the grace that God has given the Macedonian churches. Out of the most severe trial, their overflowing joy and their extreme poverty welled up in rich generosity. For I testify that they gave as much as they were able, and even beyond their ability. Entirely on their own, they urgently pleaded with us for the privilege of sharing in this service to the saints. And they did not do as we expected, but they gave themselves first to the Lord and then to us in keeping with God's will.

It is important to note the context of this particular passage. Paul was collecting money for the needy church in Jerusalem. As he traveled through Europe, specifically in the region of Macedonia, he told of the need of the fellow Christians in Jerusalem. What adds to the impact of this whole story is that Macedonia was economically depressed. Charles Swindoll says, "Macedonia was to Paul a lot like India is to us. It would be like encouraging the people of Appalachia to respond to those who are hurting in the ghetto of Harlem." Yet they did respond and gave well beyond their ability.

Notice some of the qualities that these believers manifested when it came to sacrificial giving. Giving, whether it is of ourselves or of our time, talents, or treasures, ought to take place in the following ways.

Give anonymously. One specific church is not stated in this passage. We read simply "the churches in Macedonia." There was no compelling need to be noticed. That's tough. It is not easy to serve others and not be noticed. But, true servanthood needs no recognition. In fact, it seeks not to be recognized by anyone but God who really is checking our heart and inner motives. A true servant's heart, then, is typified by anonymity.

Give generously. When the Corinthians gave they "overflowed in the process." They sacrificially gave "beyond their ability." This type of sacrificial giving is typified by Onesiphorus. He modeled tremendous generosity in his love for Paul.

Paul says in 2 Timothy 1:16-18, "May the Lord show mercy to the household of Onesiphorus, because he often refreshed me and was not ashamed of my chains. On the contrary, when he was in Rome, he searched hard for me until he found me. May the Lord grant that he will find mercy from the Lord on that day! You know very well in how many ways he helped me in Ephesus." How well does your life match up with Onesiphorus? He knew sacrificial giving. That generous giving is the same kind that God is calling you to in your mentoring relationships.

Give voluntarily. The Living Bible says, "I can testify that they did it because they wanted to, and not because of nagging on my part. They begged us to take the money so they could share in the joy of helping" (2 Corinthians 8:3-4 TLB). There is no joy in giving out of compulsion.

Obligation is a terrible motivation for giving and is a damper on receiving.

Such sacrificial giving is what God asks of you in order that you might become the kind of mentor that is needed in this day and age—a humble leader, ready and willing to serve.

## SERVANT LEADERSHIP

A servant leader does not insist on his own way or demand recognition but is teachable and reliant on God. In 1 Thessalonians 2, Paul says they 'proved to be' or 'were' a certain kind of people among the Thessalonians. In other words, Paul claims that their habitual lifestyle reflected certain kinds of positive activities and character. Paul, Timothy, and Silas acted as mature, disciplined individuals. Rather than being inconsistent, they were steady, mature models for the people of Thessalonica. The key to their ability to have this type of stability in their lifestyles was discipline.

Nancy Leigh DeMoss shares the following reflections on Ron's servant leadership in her own life. "Throughout my teenage years, Ron, along with his wife, Mary, invested in my life, building on the foundation that my parents, pastors, and others had already laid. At my request, they trained and equipped me for effective ministry. This informal 'mentoring' program took numerous forms.

"Periodically, we would meet in my home, and Ron helped me think through a biblical philosophy of ministry. It's been over thirty years now, but I still remember the things that he taught me.

"As part of a D.Min. seminary program that Ron had completed just before he came to our church, he and his wife, Mary, had spent several months traveling across the country and studying local church ministries. When they arrived in Philadelphia to serve on our church staff, their belongings included dozens of boxes of resources they had picked up from the churches they had visited. Ron assigned me the task of organizing it all and developing a filing system that I ended up using myself when I joined the staff of a local church after college. In the process of wading through all those papers, I became acquainted with and developed a heart for various aspects of local church ministry.

"Ron encouraged me to develop my understanding of ministry by getting into the Word. The first 'assignment' he gave me was to come up with a list of the characteristics of an effective minister and an effective ministry, based on 1 Thessalonians chapters one and two. That passage has since been woven into my life. It taught me the importance of living a life that is consistent with the message I proclaim, of laying down my life for those I serve, of genuine love, and of dependence on the power of God to change lives. Just the other day, when I was asked to speak 'spontaneously' to about a hundred small-group Bible study leaders, I opened my Bible to 1 Thessalonians 1 and 2, and walked through the principles I first became acquainted with some thirty years ago.

"As the apostle Paul did with the Thessalonians, Ron and Mary took me into their lives, opened their hearts and home to me, and did more training than they probably ever realized, in the context of real-life circumstances and everyday, informal interaction.

"They were encouragers of my faith and expressed interest and concern about my personal walk with God, my family life, and my relationships. They gave me perspective and counsel as I grew through those (sometimes bumpy) teenage years.

"Looking back, I'm sure I was not always sensitive to their schedules—I suspect there were times when they would have welcomed some relief from their over-eager 'shadow,' but if that was the case, they never let on.

"Through all of these experiences, I cultivated a deep love for ministry and developed tools that I have found invaluable in more than twenty-five years of vocational Christian service. Their humble servanthood gave me an opportunity to develop my God-given gifts."

### SERVING LIKE JESUS CHRIST

Michael D. Vessey says, "For nearly forty years, I have had the privilege of being mentored by Dr. Ted Engstrom. Through him, I have learned that mentoring is not simply the imparting of new skills or a program by which to lead life. Rather, it is the imparting of character and wisdom that the mentor has gained through experience."

> "Mentoring is not simply the imparting of new skills or a program by which to lead life. Rather, it is the imparting of character and wisdom that the mentor has gained through experience."

Jesus Christ's teaching went beyond pouring knowledge into the heads of his disciples. It encompassed values as well. This was not easy because the values he presented were in sharp contrast to the values of that time, even though the people of Israel had a unique opportunity to know and obey the commandments of God. Christ's men struggled constantly with Kingdom values. It's the same today. What Jesus taught often seems backward, upside down, and just the reverse of what comes naturally.

Unlike mentors who are often considered "successful" today, Jesus did not organize his team in order to be served. He never asked them to make him look good. They were never required to wait on him. Just the opposite was true: *He served them.* The Master built them up, encouraged them, corrected them, and stretched them as they struggled to receive the truth and obey the will of God.

His example can have a profound impact on our mentoring if we copy ourselves after him. Lead by serving, receive by giving, change lives through love and sacrifice. These values—though "questionable" today—are the ones that fueled Jesus' highly successful mentoring.

"Whoever wants to become great among you must be your servant, and whoever wants to be first must be slave of all" Jesus taught in Mark 10:43–45, "For even the Son of Man did not come to be served, but to serve, and to give his life as a ransom for many." In John 13:15, he said in the upper room after washing his disciples' feet, "I have set you an example that you should do as I have done for you."

Philippians 2:3–11 says:

> Do nothing out of selfish ambition or vain conceit, but in humility consider others better than yourselves. Each of you should look not only to your own interests, but also to the interests of others.

Your attitude should be the same as that of Christ Jesus: Who, being in very nature God, did not consider equality with God something to be grasped, but made himself nothing, taking the very nature of a servant, being made in human likeness. And being found in appearance as a man, he humbled himself and became obedient to death—even death on a cross! Therefore God exalted him to the highest place and gave him the name that is above every name, that at the name of Jesus every knee should bow, in heaven and on earth and under the earth, and every tongue confess that Jesus Christ is Lord, to the glory of God the Father.

May that be our example as we serve our mentorees! An attitude like Christ's, a willingness to serve, a sacrificial life, and humility, will allow us to become great biblical mentors.

## OTHER LEADERS SAY . . .

*"The giving of oneself to another in a mentoring relationship is the basis of growing the next generation of leaders. Humility, sacrificial living, and serving as our Lord Jesus did are qualities that every Christian leader should strive to attain. Servanthood in our mentoring relationships must also be intentional. We are to be developing others so they might surpass us in life and ministry. Just as Jesus said to his disciples, 'You shall do greater works than*

*I have done,' so should our empowerment be for those who are in our realm of influence.*

*"This can be done by relinquishing some of our opportunities into their hands—each time with the hope and prayer they will become greater in the work they do for Jesus than we have ever done. There is great reward in seeing them grow and launch out; our role in their life has come full cycle. Reproduction and mentoring occur through modeling and surrender on the part of the mentor. Jesus was the ultimate servant to us. We are to serve those whom he has put in our lives with similar selflessness so his kingdom might expand."*

*—MARTHA WAGNER is the founder and executive director of Hope Ministries International. She evangelizes, teaches the Bible, and mentors women in leadership both in the United States and overseas. Her latest project is writing and producing the play* Better than a Story *as an evangelistic tool to reach women in the U.S. with the message of Jesus.*

*"The authors develop the concept of servanthood in mentoring, using the words, humility, sacrificial living, and servant leadership. Additionally, they exhort you to a focus on God with compelling statements, such as, 'Humility believes that God will work through you and your gifts.'*

*"You might add that God's greatest call to you as a Christian mentor will be an abandoned love relationship with God (Matthew 22:37–38). Scripture exhorts you to continually live/walk/choose God rather than yourself*

*(Galatians 5:16). From this Spirit-empowered love relationship with Christ will flow the fruit of the Spirit (Galatians 5:22) which describes you as a servant of God and a servant of (love for) your neighbor (Matthew 22:39). The bottom line of servanthood mentoring is love—love for God and love from God to you and through you to the one mentored.*

—ALLEN H. QUIST is the president of Ministry Management Seminars and is an adjunct instructor at Multnomah Biblical Seminary in Portland, Oregon.

*"The greatest experiences of my Christian life have come to me as opportunities to serve, not 'invitations' to grow my ministry! Time and again, I remember the unexpected blessings of the Lord through serving others. As an evangelist, D. L. Moody has obviously been a 'magnet' must-read for me. After high school, I dreamed of attending Moody Bible Institute. Think of it, small town, little ole me walking in the wake of this evangelical giant. However, inadequate grades kept me from attending. In my twenties a trip to Chicago allowed me to visit the institute and historic Moody Church, where my friend Dr. Erwin Lutzer now pastors. My wife took a picture of me behind the pulpit. I was awed by the historical richness of the church. In fact, after the picture, I prayed, 'Lord, if it's your will, please allow me to speak in this magnificent place.'*

*"Now twenty years later, I remember visiting Moody Broadcasting to record a radio program with Wayne Shepherd, grab a quick cup of coffee, attend chapel at the institute, and go home. That's when the invitation to*

serve happened! On the way to historic Torrey-Gray Auditorium, then acting President Dr. Joseph Stowell caught me off guard with the words, 'Silva, my friend, God has a wonderful plan for your life, and I'm going to tell you what it is!' It was a Tuesday—that's President's chapel day at Moody. An immediate unexpected situation was calling Dr. Stowell out of town. 'Silva,' he continued, 'if you have ever wanted to help me, now is the time!' I do not remember my message on that day, the clothes I was wearing, or the brand of coffee I enjoyed with Wayne, but I have lived the principle Dr. Engstrom and Dr. Jenson teach in this chapter. I know experientially that it's true and it works: the most wonderful opportunities in the Kingdom are often presented to us as simple invitations to serve someone around you."

—MIKE SILVA *is an international missionary evangelist who specializes in difficult, out-of-the-way places where the gospel is richly received. More information about his ministry and new book* Seeing is Believing *are available at www.mikesilva.org.*

"Servant Leadership seems to be a conflicting term at first glance. Certainly as the world looks at leadership, especially in a business environment, it is about leadership not being a servant.

"Christ set the example for us in all areas of being a leader. He provided the great example and boldly asked others to follow. It is interesting to note that when the disciples entered the room for that last dinner together they did not offer to wash the feet of the others as was the custom. Instead Jesus gets up from the table and humbly washes their feet. So often we look at demean-

*ing work and feel that surely someone else should be doing that.*

*"I have known about World Vision since I was in college. I have the highest respect for what they do and who they are. I did not have the privilege of meeting Dr. Ted Engstrom until two years ago when my mother moved to the same retirement center where Dr. Engstrom lives with his wife. I saw him in a very different setting. How humble he was as he interacted with the residents there. This man of great leadership who was responsible for a large budget and many tasks now lives simply in a Christ-like way quietly serving his wife and those around him.*

*"Dr. Ron Jenson and I met on an international speaking tour several years ago. I had been building networks internationally for many years and was convinced that without showing servant leadership to people of many cultures it was impossible to meet the many needs represented in each places. One day as we were being transported from the hotel where the speakers were staying I happened to be in the same car with Ron. My son was with me on this trip. Ron immediately began to talk to him and encourage him in his goals and plans for the future. Later when I saw him speak to a crowd of several thousand I remembered his kind words to my son. He was the same man off stage and on stage. This means a great deal when you see many who are glorious in their presentation in front of people and quite different one on one. Ron lives what he speaks about.*

*"He has encouraged me many times to think bigger and expand the heavenly vision. 'For to me to live is Christ'*

*is his theme. Often he has spoken for leadership groups in my business. They always come away better for having been under his teaching."*

—BEVERLY SALLEE is a global businesswoman who endeavors to engage business people in charitable projects in their region through her marketing business, Premier Training Concepts.

*"In reading this chapter, I was impressed with the simple phrase the authors use to describe Jesus Christ's example to us: 'Lead by serving.' Christ served thousands of needy people in His three short years of public ministry: teaching, healing, feeding, and caring (see Acts 10:38). And who witnessed his ministry? His disciples. One of the ways he trained them was by living out true servanthood. He obeyed the Father by serving those around him, and in the process he developed his disciples. We read in the book of Acts how they devoted their lives to ministering to people. Christ was the perfect servant. He exemplified 'Lifestyle Servanthood.'*

*"Ted and Ron remind us of what the apostle Paul says: 'Let this mind be in you which was also in Christ Jesus' (Phil. 2:5). In following Christ's example, we will, in the course of life, serve others. The discerning among them will follow our leading and learn lessons from our attitude toward service. I recall a gifted preacher who didn't limit his service to the pulpit. He didn't think it beneath him to help set up the chairs for the next meeting. He would cheerfully vacuum the sanctuary carpet or water the flowers. Was he mentoring me? Yes. He was showing me how to serve God and his people in menial, modest, quiet ways. He taught me a lesson about humble service.*

*If we truly want to mentor others, let us exhibit 'lifestyle servanthood.'"*

> —ROB TYLER is director of ECS Ministries, distributor of over a million Bible correspondence courses a year worldwide, and publisher of Christian books and group study guides (www.ecsministries.org).

*"As I was digesting this chapter, I was reading the book of Nehemiah in my devotions. Nehemiah was leading the Israelites in the rebuilding of the walls of Jerusalem. Chapter 3 lists all the priests, individuals, families and clans and what part of the wall they were responsible to rebuild. But verse 5 jumped out at me, especially in this context of servanthood: "The next section was repaired by the men of Tekoa, but their nobles would not put their shoulders to the work under their supervisors." Priests, goldsmiths, sons, grandsons, and even perfume makers were building their section of the wall, but the leaders from Tekoa refused to help.*

*"I am blessed to serve with a great group of servants at Gospel Communications, and I hope they have learned what I have tried to model: I will never ask them to do something I am unwilling to do myself. Christ's example is clear. We just have to keep our egos out of the way."*

> —J. R. WHITBY serves as president and CEO of Gospel Communications International (www.gospelcom.net).

## HOW ABOUT YOU?

Determine your level of proficiency in the area of servanthood from the chart below. 1 is the lowest, 10 is the highest with 5 as average.

## SERVANTHOOD

| 1 | 1.5 | 2 | 2.5 | 3 | 3.5 | 4 | 4.5 | 5 | 5.5 | 6 | 6.5 | 7 | 7.5 | 8 | 8.5 | 9 | 9.5 | 10 |
|---|-----|---|-----|---|-----|---|-----|---|-----|---|-----|---|-----|---|-----|---|-----|----|

What do you need to do in order to improve half of a point this week in your mentoring relationships?

*"Being a Christian is more than just an instantaneous conversion—it is a daily process whereby you grow to be more and more like Christ. Jesus Christ is the man God wants every man to be like."*

–BILLY GRAHAM

*"The most godly Christian is the one who knows himself best, and no one who knows himself will believe that he deserves anything better than hell."*

–A. W. TOZER

# Chapter 8

# GODLINESS

M oses was certainly a godly man. After his unique calling by God in the burning bush, he went to Egypt to assist in the Exodus of God's people, the Israelites. He also put up with millions of whiners in the desert and continued to advocate to God for them. Moses brought the covenant and the law to the people. He was a prophet and leader and he spoke to God face-to-face. It's hard to top that résumé!

Moses was also a mentor. His successor, Joshua, was one of the twelve spies who assessed the Promised Land before the Israelites moved in (and before their forty years of wandering in the desert). The Lord told Moses, "Commission Joshua, and encourage and strengthen him, for he will lead this people across and will cause them to inherit the land that you will see" (Deuteronomy 3:28). Joshua's strength and skill as a leader was largely influenced by Moses' godliness. Moses' life was an example of holy living and his treatment of Joshua was in line with God's commands.

Joshua went on to lead the Israelites into the Promised Land, defeat the enemies who possessed the land, and divide the land among the twelve tribes. He earned the respect of the people and the support of God in all he did. This godly leader, Joshua, was shaped by his mentor and another godly leader, Moses.

Godliness is the greatest asset a mentor can possess. When God's people are seeking to be like him, he supports that desire by producing godliness in their lives. The Holy Spirit's main role in our lives is to remind us of Jesus' teachings and produce the fruit of the Spirit in our lives.

> When God's people are seeking to be like him, he supports that desire by producing godliness in their lives.

The fruit of the Spirit is "love, joy, peace, patience, kindness, goodness, faithfulness, gentleness, and self-control." The apostle Paul reminds us that "since we live by the Spirit (as Christians), let us keep in step with the Spirit" (Galatians 5:22–23). The Holy Spirit is also called the Counselor. His role is to teach us and remind us of Jesus' words. This counsel and indwelling enables us to produce good fruit—the fruit of the Holy Spirit.

## NO BASIS FOR REPROACH

The apostle Paul gives us a glimpse into what godliness should look like today. First Thessalonians 2:10 says, "You are witnesses, and so is God, of how holy, righteous, and blameless we were among you who believed." Paul was saying in essence that there was no basis for reproach by God or man in the relationships that Paul, Timothy, and Silas had with the Thessalonians.

Paul was not saying that they were perfect. He was claiming that their efforts to seek the good of the Thessalonians were so sincere that no reproach could be brought against them or their message. These men sought to behave appropriately before God. They acknowledged that God knew their thoughts, their attitudes, their feelings, and their motives. They fully understood that they could hide nothing from God. And they lived holy, godly lives in light of that understanding.

Godliness is the capstone attribute of an effective Christian mentor. Godliness is the common theme behind each mentoring characteristic we have covered

**Godliness is being like God in thought and behavior. It is a way of living and a way of viewing the world and other people.**

so far. A godly mentor already possesses many of the necessary skills, habits, and attributes so essential to good mentoring. Godliness is being like God in thought and behavior. It is a way of living and a way of viewing the world and other people. Let's explore the elements that contribute to the making of a godly life.

## PATTERN OF HOLINESS

The first element of godliness is holy living. A sinful lifestyle is not a godly lifestyle. Therefore, the pursuit of holiness in every area of your life will help you to become more godly. First Timothy 4:7–12 and 16 says:

> Have nothing to do with godless myths and old wives' tales; rather, train yourself to be godly. For physical training is of some value, but godliness has value for all things, holding promise for both the present life and the life to come.
>
> This is a trustworthy saying that deserves

full acceptance (and for this we labor and strive), that we have put our hope in the living God, who is the Savior of all men, and especially of those who believe.

Command and teach these things. Don't let anyone look down on you because you are young, but set an example for the believers in speech, in life, in love, in faith, and in purity. . . . Watch your life and doctrine closely. Persevere in them, because if you do, you will save both yourself and your hearers.

This passage gives us incredible insight into what godliness really is. First, it tells us that godliness requires training much as marathon running requires training. While physical training only lasts as long as the body is well and able, godliness training will last for eternity ("the present life and the life to come").

Next, Paul tells his young mentoree, Timothy, that he should not allow other Christians to look down on him. Rather, his life should be so godly that they take their cues from him and follow his lead. Timothy is instructed to set a godly example in speech, in life, in love, in faith, in purity, and in doctrine. His godliness in these areas will mean life for himself—and his hearers (i.e. his mentorees!).

Timothy's life and habits were modeled after Paul's godliness. In addition, Timothy's life and godly habits were influencing the people that he was teaching and leading. Paul's godliness was sure to continue its influence, even in places that he was not directly ministering, *because his godliness had changed Timothy's life.*

We too can extend our circle of impact to include all those people who are mentored by those whom we mentor. In our mentoring relationships, therefore, it is essential that we build on a foundation of godliness.

## LEADING BY EXAMPLE

Titus 2:7-8 says, "In everything set them an example by doing what is good. In your teaching show integrity, seriousness and soundness of speech that cannot be condemned." Here, Paul is addressing one of his other mentorees, Titus. He gives Titus a similar message to the one that he has given Timothy: set an example by your godliness so that others may follow your lead. Integrity and consistency in holy living, seriousness about the things of God, correct speech and teaching: these things cannot be looked down on. Titus will lead by example (even if he is not intentionally leading) if he lives a godly life.

Your character, not curriculum or programs, inspires the mentoree to become more Christ-like. Books, articles, conferences, and church services are helpful for growth in the Christian walk for your mentoree. But it is your character that can literally shape your mentoree's own character. If you are godly, your mentoree will probably be godly too.

Near the end of my (Ron) cross-country trip to interview ministry leaders, I visited Arrowhead Springs and Bill Bright, founder and president of Campus Crusade for Christ. That visit in 1974 was the first time I had seen him since the 1960s. We had just visited with and interviewed the top Christian leaders in the country. We asked them pointed questions about their ministries, and they responded with great stories. Then, we asked Bill about his incredible ministry, Campus Crusade for Christ International, and all he talked about, with tears running down his cheeks, was Jesus. His godly attitude was an example to me that continues even though he has gone home to be with the Lord.

An unknown writer has penned, "The measure of man's real character is what he would do if he knew he would never be found out." What would you do if you knew you would never get caught? Would you still lead a holy, blameless life in order to please God (who always "finds out")? Then your character measures up, you are living in godliness. This is not to say that you are literally blameless, but that your life is centered and grounded upon righteous living.

Susan Henson says about her mentor, Nancy Leigh DeMoss, "Her passion to know God and his Word and her walk in light of those truths kindles a love flame that is contagious and is ever spreading. John Maxwell said, 'We can teach what we know, but we reproduce what we are.' Nancy's 'life-on-life' mentorship has set me on a course seeking an intimate relationship with God that has transformed my life and ministry." Nancy's godliness has spilled into Susan's life, giving her a desire to seek God and minister to those around her out of love.

> "We can **teach** what we know, but we **reproduce** what we are."

## "FOLLOW ME AS I FOLLOW CHRIST"

First Corinthians 11:1 says, "Follow my example, as I follow the example of Christ." Can you imagine telling other people that they are to follow you? Paul's confidence in this statement does not come from his own good deeds or blameless life. His confidence comes from his own mentor, Jesus Christ. Jesus' life and work are our perfect example.

Why did Paul make this strong statement to the Corinthians? He knew the power of example, and he knew what modeling could do. He was ministering to a group of new Christians (the Corinthian church) who desperately needed a picture of what the Christian life ought to be. Paul knew that they would ultimately become like the people around them, especially their leaders. Therefore, Paul insisted that Christians, especially those in leadership positions, be godly models.

You too must buy into the power of modeling. Whether you like it or not, you are a witness (a model). Your protégés are watching you as an example of what they should be. Can you say along with Paul, "Follow me, as I follow Christ Jesus"?

As in Paul's day, people around you are watching you and will consciously or unconsciously emulate your behavior. Philippians 3:17 says, "Join with others in following my example, brothers, and take note of those who live according to the pattern we gave you." Philippians 4:9 says, "Whatever you have learned or received or heard from me, or seen in me—put it into practice. And the God of peace will be with you." What will the results be when your mentoree follows your example as you follow Christ's example? He will become like Christ, he will display the fruits of the Spirit, and his heart will be after God's own heart.

The basis for telling others to follow you is not pride or a wrong self-concept. It is a deep trust that you know

> A life **patterned** after Christ's is **godly** in the fullest sense. Without being prideful, we can boast of what **God has done** in our hearts and lives.

where you are going and what you are doing because you are pressing forward after Christ's example. A life patterned after Christ's is godly in the fullest sense. Without being prideful, we can boast of what God has done in our hearts and lives. Let your mentoree see such a godly example that she is compelled to follow your pattern for holy living.

### POINT PEOPLE TO GOD, NOT YOU

Godliness is a model for the mentoree and ultimately directs people to God, not to the mentor. If your goal in mentoring is to see your protégé become just like you, then you have a skewed aim. Instead, your goal should be to see your mentoree reach her full potential and become Christ-like.

Anne Sire Greenquist says about her mentor, Beverly Sallee, "Beverly has given me a healthy perspective on how to move my eyes away from myself and to center on Christ. And knowing the huge impact Beverly has had in my life, I look forward to today and tomorrow where I can be reaching out to others who need the same positive influence in their lives."

Beverly's godly impact in Anne's life gives her the desire to impact others in the same way. Beverly's desire was not for Anne to become a little "Beverly," but that Anne might realize all that God has created her to be.

## TEACHABILITY

Bobb Biehl gives the following advice to mentors, "*Be teachable.* This might sound odd as a prerequisite for being a good mentor because it's the *protégé's* job to learn from you. But I have found that if I remain teachable, then I am modeling the teachability which I want my protégé to have. You can learn from everyone. What's more, I've found that as a mentor pours himself into a person and gives and gives and gives, sooner or later that person in whom he has invested so much will want to give him something back.

"If . . . I can learn from you, then suddenly it's a two-way street. The protégé says, 'Hey, my mentor respects me' (and vice versa). If the mentor remains teachable, it shows that he really does admire his protégé and believes in his future."

In godliness, no one is an expert. Therefore, it is to your profit to remain teachable and open to what your mentoree can teach you. Perhaps they have a deep sense of compassion or they are exceptionally generous. Let them "mentor" or teach you as well, so that you might both become more godly through the other person's impact.

> A godly mentor is **above** reproach and has a **pattern** of holiness set **deep** in his life.

A godly mentor is above reproach and has a pattern of holiness set deep in his life. Holy living means that you are fit to lead by example as you follow the example of Jesus Christ. As a godly mentor, you must also have the humility to acknowledge that you are not perfect. You can point your protégé to Christ as their ultimate example.

The overarching qualities of a godly mentor are teachability and a willingness to let the Holy Spirit change you. These elements of godliness will set a course of righteous, full living for your own life. In addition, your mentoree will see firsthand the way to live as Christ would in his workplace, home, church, and community. Godly living reaps the fruit of love, joy, peace, patience, kindness, goodness, faithfulness, gentleness, and self-control in your own life and in your protégé's life!

## OTHER LEADERS SAY . . .

*"There's an old saying, 'You can only export what you grow at home.' Do you want to be a mentor? First, take a good look at the fruit being produced in your own life. Does your life reflect more of the godliness of Jesus or does it more closely resemble the world? What you read, watch, listen to, and the actions you take (especially when no else is looking) are the true tests of your character. The word 'disciple' implies a student 'disciplining his life' to become like his teacher. The longer and more intensely a disciple is under your instruction, the more they will begin to take on your character and personality; likewise, the longer and more intensely you fellowship with the Lord, through his Word and prayer, the more you will become like him. The apostle Peter told us that in God's Word we are given great and precious promises. Through these promises we will acquire more of his nature and personality to escape sinful temptation (2 Peter 1:4). The Word also says, 'Without holiness, not one will see the Lord' (Hebrews 12:14).*

*"True godliness is a daily walk with God, a daily crucifying of your fleshly sinful desires and selfish ambitions. Paul said, 'I die daily' (1 Corinthians 15:31). He also said, 'I have been crucified with Christ, but nevertheless I live, yet it is not I that live, but Christ who lives within me' (Galatians 2:20). Godliness is a daily walk, desiring to please him, and being quick to repent if a failure is made."*

—JON DUNAGAN is a missionary evangelist. For nearly twenty years he has been preaching in remote cities and villages where Jesus Christ had not yet been publicly proclaimed. His travels have taken him to every continent, including Antarctica. He is happily married and the proud father of seven godly children.

*"Ted and Ron concisely highlight the most significant godliness concept that any mentor could remember: "In godliness, no one is an expert." This means, that when I invite a person to "follow me" I must be willing to own my influence, not just my words. Therefore, my mentoring model changes from one of holding people accountable for what I tell them, to giving myself to them, like Jesus did. Giving myself in an authentic 'follow me' relationship means I give the person not only my strengths but my weaknesses, not only my hopes but my fears, not only my successes but my failures, not only what I know, but who I am. I live before them with nothing hidden. Why? So the follower can see the actual process—often in contrast to the stated process—of me learning to live out of who God says I am."*

—BILL THRALL, BRUCE MCNICOL, and JOHN LYNCH are the co-authors of the acclaimed books *The Ascent of a Leader, Beyond Your Best,* and *TrueFaced.*

*"Walking the path toward godliness is a never ending ex-
perience and a soul-satisfying journey. Recently, I thought
of the awesome reality of being created in the image of
God. It occurred to me a key factor is God's gift of volition,
or free will choice. Amazingly I possess total, final and
perfect control over the very next thought I permit to enter
my mind. To receive or reject it is my choice and mine
alone. Because of my sinful nature, I need the counsel of
the Spirit of Truth, the Holy Spirit. So I began praying
this life-changing prayer every day and throughout the
day. 'Father, please stand guard with me at the doorway
of my mind and do not permit any thought to enter that is
not blessed by you and bring into my mind those thoughts
that place me in the center of your will.' This spiritual
discipline is becoming a life-changing experience."*

—JIM RUSSELL is the founder and president of The Amy
Foundation (www.amyfound.org).

*"Godliness is indeed 'the capstone attribute of an effec-
tive Christian mentor.' But even more, it is also an objective to be pursued continuously above all others. We are
not born with it—in fact our nature fights against developing it. Every person that is committed to Jesus Christ
is a mentor—for better or worse. We become a 'lightning
rod' to those around us, Christian and non-Christian
alike; ergo, our responsibility is to continuously develop
(with the power and guidance of the Holy Spirit) our
mentoring attributes to become more effective. The New
Testament mentor model is not something to 'buy into,' it
is an example that should be embraced with enthusiasm,
as second nature to a young or mature Christian as putting on a coat. The mentor/mentoree relationship is built*

*fundamentally on trust—crucially, accountability must be an integral component. By definition, a person is in a mentoring relationship to learn from a more mature and wise person. This does not preclude or exclude the potential that the mentor may also learn and grow by this process. In fact, a good mentor will (as stated earlier) continuously grow as he or she pursues godliness. However, there is a special quality of humbleness and respect that the mentoree should exercise that is very much like a relationship in teaching music. In my experience, both as a student at Juilliard and teacher at other schools, I found that humbleness and respect were attributes that were not all that common. My teacher told me one day that it was important for me to take her ideas and work with them to learn as much as possible. Then later, when I no longer was studying with her I could develop my own ideas. In effect, I, the mentoree, would become the mentor. I found that students who did not embrace the ideas of her teaching also did not learn and grow. There is a misconception that to be mentored means that you will become a clone of the mentor. A good teacher/mentor will not make carbon-copies of himself or herself, but will point the student/mentoree towards a worthy goal. In the case of a Christian mentor, that goal is pursuing continuously the fruits of the Holy Spirit."*

—PETER KENOTE, DMA, is a violist with the New York Philharmonic. He teaches viola privately and is a husband and a father to three wonderful daughters.

*"Over the years, I have known many talented, bright, charismatic individuals with impressive credentials and accomplishments. But the people who have made an*

*indelible impression on my life—the ones I am drawn to like a magnet, those I desire to emulate—are the men and women I would describe as godly. Those individuals have not all been impressive or successful in the world's eyes, but they have made me thirsty to know God and to walk with him more closely.*

*"Godliness can't be quantified or measured in a test tube. It is the gracious, winsome fruit of a heart that is intentional and persistent about seeking after God, the fragrance of a life lived supremely for his pleasure and glory. When it's all said and done—when friends and family stand by my grave—I don't want to be remembered as a best-selling author or spell-binding speaker. My prayer is that people will say, 'She was a godly woman.' Then my life will have fulfilled its mission—to point people to God."*

—NANCY LEIGH DEMOSS is the author of many books, including *Seeking Him: Experiencing the Joy of Personal Revival*. She is the host of *Revive Our Hearts* radio.

## HOW ABOUT YOU?

Determine your level of proficiency in the area of godliness from the chart below. 1 is the lowest, 10 is the highest with 5 as average.

## GODLINESS

| 1 | 1.5 | 2 | 2.5 | 3 | 3.5 | 4 | 4.5 | 5 | 5.5 | 6 | 6.5 | 7 | 7.5 | 8 | 8.5 | 9 | 9.5 | 10 |
|---|-----|---|-----|---|-----|---|-----|---|-----|---|-----|---|-----|---|-----|---|-----|----|

What do you need to do in order to improve half of a point this week in your mentoring relationships?

*"An unexamined life is not worth living."*
–SOCRATES


*"Perhaps the main task of the minister is to prevent people from suffering for the wrong reasons. Many people suffer because of the false supposition on which they have based their lives. That supposition is that there should be no fear or loneliness, no confusion or doubt. But these sufferings can only be dealt with creatively when they are understood as wounds integral to our human condition. Therefore ministry is a very confronting service. It does not allow people to live with illusions of immortality and wholeness. It keeps reminding others that they are mortal and broken, but also that with the recognition of this condition, liberation starts."*
–HENRI NOUWEN

# Chapter 9
# CONFRONTATION

**S**ome time ago, I (Ron) was called by the pastor of a mega-church. The pastor is a friend of mine and said, "We're ready to implode. You need to help mentor us through this." I spent two days with them and had all of the executive committee together. The church was growing but had a "military general" for a pastor. They needed to become a team.

There were seven or eight pastors in leadership at the church. I met separately with each one of them. I asked them what the issues were. Then we all met together and I asked the group what the issues were. At the beginning of the meeting, I laid out the twelve steps to conflict resolution. Everyone agreed there were problems. Specifically, they were having trouble with the executive pastor, who was raised in a "stiff" culture and was used to running things that way. The senior pastor tended to micromanage and get angry. Another pastor tried to create codependency by making people feel good without solving the problems.

Over a twelve-hour period of time, the whole group discussed the issues. At the end, everyone asked for and gave forgiveness. That was three years ago. The church staff is now completely healed. They have started to listen and understand communication.

The church staff was afraid to confront. That is often true in many settings, including the corporate and ministry worlds. Real communication and confrontation can be very scary—but it is also healing and rewarding!

The mentor who sees his charge stumble must invade that person's private world. Change will most likely never happen unless that is done. Confrontation has a vital part to play in the mentoring relationship: it allows healing, restoration, growth and, ultimately, victory.

Alan Hlavka is a pastor in Boring, Oregon. One of his mentorees shares with us his experience of confrontation with Alan. "God has made an amazing transformation in my life over the past year. It was not possible for me to conceive of this just fourteen months ago. I was clueless to the impending 'crashing down to rock bottom' event that lay just ahead.

"My wife and I had been quite active in ministry to young couples in our church and were preparing to take on the role of Lead Shepherds to a 'mini-church' (a small church within our larger body) comprised of couples in their twenties to forties. I had also been leading a men's accountability group with many of the guys from this mini-church.

"Two of our elders, including Alan, invited me to meet with them at church. Over the past several years I had been in contact with both men, and I enjoyed their teaching both from the pulpit as well as the occasional visit to our mini-church. Still, I was a bit apprehensive as to what they wanted to discuss. I waited nervously in the lobby for a few minutes until Alan came out to greet me and usher me to the office. These were men for whom I have deep respect, and I was humbled to learn that I was being asked to consider joining them as shepherding elders of our church. After talking about the responsibility of this position, I agreed to talk with my wife and to pray about it.

"I travel a great deal for my work as a national account manager, and occasionally have opportunity to entertain clients at various dinners and events. Although I had made a commitment to always have integrity in these activities, I recently had made an extremely poor (meaning sinful and stupid) choice to accompany some men to an inappropriate venue. This was not the first time for me to fall in sexual sin, but it was an area of sin that I thought that I had mastery over. As I prayed about the elder nomination, the Holy Spirit made it abundantly clear that I must confess to Alan and the other pastor. I had too much respect for them to be less than fully honest.

"Shortly thereafter I found myself confessing this sin that had haunted me for years to a man that I deeply respect, Alan Hlavka. That was tough, but now came the true test of manhood: confessing to my wife. Alan wouldn't let me off the hook, but provided the support and encouragement that I needed.

"It was a Monday morning, and I stayed home from work to share with my wife. As we talked, the full weight of my sin hit in a crushing blow. God used my wife's enormous grief to provide a vivid picture of how he sees sin. The ensuing brokenness in my life was too great for me to bear alone.

"It was at this point that God used Alan to begin a process of healing in my marriage and in my personal relationship with my heavenly Father. At just the right moments, when my wife or I needed encouragement,

Alan would call. He prayed with us, counseled us, encouraged us, and held me accountable. We were asked to step back from ministry to allow God to heal our marriage, and to dig down and root out this sin from my life. This really hurt my wife since she hadn't done anything to 'deserve' this.

"What was Alan's response? He said, 'This is the painful part of being one flesh. When sin enters a marriage, both the husband and the wife are affected.' With sincerity and compassion, Alan spoke truth into our lives. Over time this developed a unity in our marriage that we never thought was possible.

"Alan challenged me to get below the surface. He shared some words that caused me to think hard about all the ways in which I allowed sin to creep into my life: 'a man doesn't fall in a moment.' What a weighty statement! Together we looked at God's standard for men, and what impact that standard has on marriage. What choices was I making—every day, hour, and minute—that either brought me closer to or further from overt sin?

"He also had the wisdom to know that courage and discipline were not enough to win the war of sexual purity. Alan showed me what it meant to have Christ in me, to let Christ live through me. Without this powerful change in my life, encouraged from my mentor and friend, my own personal ability to live righteously would have given out long ago. Alan helped me to understand what Paul meant when he said, 'For when I am weak, then I am strong.' There is no ability in my flesh to do good, but Christ in me can live a lifetime of purity.

"God in his glory used Alan to touch many others through my life. Not only did I confess to my wife, but to the mini-church leadership team. That spurred a few men to come forward and work through similar issues with their wives. Then I shared with more than twenty guys in the men's group that I had been leading. Many of those men saw the brokenness and pain, the result of sin when it comes to fruition, and determined to confront the sexual sin in their own lives. Later I shared the victory over this sin that God had provided with over three hundred fifty men in my church. Several of them had hope for the first time, seeing that God can provide victory in this difficult area. There were others, businessmen, co-workers, college friends. All were impacted by the Holy Spirit's work in my life through Alan Hlavka.

"My wife and I have had the privilege of caring for hurting couples in a similar way that Alan came alongside and cared for us. What a joy to be able to pass on what was entrusted to us, what was modeled for us. Not a day goes by that I do not reflect on how our ministry has changed as a result of God's work in our marriage over the past year.

"I look back on Alan's impact on my life with astonishment at the way that God can make something good out of what was meant for evil. Alan could have cast me aside as just one more casualty. Instead, he was God's craftsman who took a broken vessel and fashioned it into something of value for the Kingdom. Isn't that what a mentor does: molds, shapes, challenges and encourages?"

This man was profoundly influenced by Alan because, as a good mentor, Alan befriended him, loved him assertively, and patiently shaped, challenged, and encouraged him. Alan saw the value of continuing his mentoring relationship with him all the way through until he was able to mentor others.

Confrontation has a distinct place and role in the mentoring process. A mentor who is willing to lovingly confront sin must take measures to safeguard herself and the relationship. Confrontation can only be successfully done in a context of deep care and respect.

> Good mentors **love** their protégés assertively and **patiently** shape, challenge, and encourage them.

When should you confront? Confronting a mentoree with his or her wrong should only be done in a safe environment in which both people feel comfortable. It should only take place in private. Allow yourself plenty of time to discuss and think through the issue at hand.

Whom do you confront? Only those with whom you have a trusting, stable relationship will be good candidates for confrontation. In the mentoring relationship, it is equally appropriate for the mentor and the mentoree to confront one another. However, it is essential that confrontation only takes place after much prayer and careful thinking—it cannot be treated lightly or it will have a negative impact.

How do you confront? Use gentle words that do not accuse or blame. Speak thoughtfully and expect to answers questions and "defend" your position. If possible, limit your confrontation to the main issue and do not bring up lesser, side problems. Those can wait for another time.

Don't be surprised if your confrontation is met with hostility or denial. Likewise, be prepared to encourage your mentoree if he responds with humility and a willingness to change. Regardless of his response, you should confront with love and prayer.

What should happen after confrontation? If your mentoree is willing, make a plan to deal with the issues. Let her think of ways to eliminate trouble areas or strengthen weak areas. Take time to communicate your care through your encouraging words and offers to help. Pray with your mentoree at the close of your time together. Ask God to give both of you wisdom in becoming Christ-like.

> Take time to communicate your care through your encouraging words and offers to help.

### PROPER CONFRONTATION

Richard H. Tyre believes that one sure indication of a "toxic" mentor is someone who takes every opportunity to criticize. This person believes that mentoring is a license to point out mistakes. They may give their protégé responsibility (often too much, too soon), and then criticize them for their inexperience or mistakes. Such a mentor keeps his mentoree as a subordinate.

This is not the kind of confrontation that we are promoting. Nor is it biblical. Critical words do not communicate deep care and concern. Likewise, mistakes can only be pointed out in the context of affection and respect. Caring confrontation has a place in the mentoring relationship and can be used for the good of both the mentoree and mentor.

As mentors, we must develop the courage and the right motive to confront. For the good of the protégé and for the good of the Church, "Love must be sincere. Hate what is evil; cling to what is good. Be devoted to one another in brotherly love. Honor one another above yourselves. Never be lacking in zeal, but keep your spiritual fervor, serving the Lord" (Romans 12:9–11).

Proverbs 27:5–6 says, "Better is open rebuke than hidden love. Wounds from a friend can be trusted, but an enemy multiplies kisses." Second Timothy 4:2 says, "Preach the Word; be prepared in season and out of season; correct, rebuke and encourage—with great patience and careful instruction." First Thessalonians 5:14 says, "And we urge you, brothers, warn those who are idle, encourage the timid, help the weak, be patient with everyone." The Scriptures are clear—a healthy mentoring relationship involves a willingness to caringly confront when necessary.

Why is it so hard to confront someone? Often fear is the overriding reason that we avoid confronting others. There's the fear of rejection, no matter on which side of the confrontation you sit. You may fear being misunderstood, or that you'll hurt someone, or that you'll be so angry you will say things you don't really mean. But caring confrontation is vital to our healthy relationships with others.

Paul cared enough about those to whom he ministered to confront them in a caring way. In 1 Thessalonians 2:11 Paul talks about how he, Silas, and Timothy related to the new Christians at Thessalonica: "For you know that we dealt with each of you as a father deals with his own children."

The attitude here is one of long-suffering in view of the difficulties and problems that are common to all people. Often when we see people who are struggling in areas where we do not, our tendency is to be impatient with them in their rate of spiritual growth. The same impatience carried to an extreme is seen in people who see any struggle as unacceptable to God.

Paul speaks strongly against this kind of attitude. You ought not to be surprised when sinners sin. You should not be surprised when people do not gain instant victory in their Christian lives. Instead, you must realize that it is only by the grace of God that you make any progress; and you are to extend the same grace in being long-suffering toward those around you. Confrontation with our mentorees requires that we view them as brothers and sisters in Christ—as people of worth in the sight of God.

**Maturity** is the ability to know how to **consistently** use the **right** method at the **right** time with the **right** person.

Do you see the need for different approaches to different people at different times? Maturity is the ability to know how to consistently use the right method at the right time with the right person. This takes practice!

The New Testament writers used many words to explain confrontation: instruct (Romans 15:14), refute (Titus 1:9), discipline (Revelation 3:19), rebuke (2 Timothy 4:2), and warn (1 Thessalonians 5:14). These are words that communicate seeing a problem in the life of someone and trying to restore them through very strong urging.

These words do not imply a false judgment. God never intends us to look at someone and to make a negative judgment about their lives. God does intend for us to discern problems and even sin in the lives of other individuals and to address it. But we are not to be involved in making quick opinions based on hearsay, talking about others behind their backs, or questioning peoples' motives. Nor are we to attack every tiny fault we see. We are to discern problems in the lives of people and help them deal with those problems. This involves specifically spelling out the problem along with the solution.

PROCESS OF CONFRONTATION

The Bible lays out clear guidelines for the process of confrontation. Galatians 6:1–2 says, "Brothers, if someone is caught in a sin, you who are spiritual should restore him gently. But watch yourself, or you also may be tempted. Carry each other's burdens, and in this way you will fulfill the law of Christ."

Matthew 18:15–17 says, "If your brother sins against you, go and show him his fault, just between the two of you. If he listens to you, you have won your brother over. But if he will not listen, take one or two others along, so that 'every matter may be established by the testimony of two or three witnesses.' If he refuses to listen to them, tell it to the church; and if he refuses to listen even to the church, treat him as you would a pagan or a tax collector." The Bible says that we are to be prayerful, personal, positive, and practical in confrontation. Let's look at these one at a time.

*Prayerfully:* Pray that God will deal with sin in your own life and that he will make you pure of heart before you approach your mentoree. Also, pray that God will prepare him before you talk about his problem area. Mentors must confront prayerfully above all.

*Personally:* If you have a problem with an individual, go directly to him. Don't admonish in a crowd; you must confront alone. Confrontation must be done between those with a relationship for the purpose of restoration and growth. If the personal approach doesn't work, refer to Matthew 18:15–17 (above) for instruction.

*Positively:* When you confront, also mention positive things that you see in her life and tell her how much you appreciate her. *Then* talk about the problem that you see. In order to have an open door with your mentoree in the future, you must communicate your knowledge and appreciation of her positive qualities, even while you disapprove of her negative qualities.

*Practically:* Don't just tell someone that there is a problem in general sense. Be as specific and clear as possible. Suggest an alternative or a solution to the problem. Give him practical handles on what is wrong and what he can do to deal with the problem.

You must care enough to confront. Lives are dramatically changed when people care enough to point out weaknesses in others' lives *for their benefit.* Though confrontation is almost always painful initially, God uses it to build us into the men and women he designed us to be.

> Lives are dramatically changed when people care enough to point out weaknesses in others' lives for their benefit.

## ACCOUNTABILITY

A mentor who has the ability to impact the whole world is one who understands accountability, and one whose life is open to a few trusted confidants, and who demands of protégés the same appraisal. A good mentor believes Matthew 12:36, "But I tell you that men will have to give account on the day of judgment for every careless word they have spoken."

Each person gives an account for himself or herself, not for anyone else. Romans 14:11–12 reminds us that "It is written: 'As surely as I live,' says the Lord, 'every knee will bow before me; every tongue will confess to God.'" So then, each of us will give an account of ourself to God.

Is someone accountable to you so that you can make him accountable to God? Can you name one or more people outside your family to whom you have made yourself accountable? Are you aware of the dangers of unaccountability—dangers such as blind spots, unhealthy relationships, and unspoken motives—that will never be known without such a friend? When was the last time that you gave an account for the private areas of your life to someone outside your family? These would include your finances, occupational diligence or lack of it, your attitude at the office, or packing too many hours of work into each day. How about an appraisal of your friendships? Or your struggle with besetting sins?

When Joseph was in the house of Potiphar, he was accountable to him. Even when Potiphar's wife made those unwise advances on the innocent man and later screamed rape, Joseph was accountable to Potiphar.

When Saul became king, he was in a hurry for the prophet Samuel to arrive so an offering could be made. Samuel was late, so Saul took matters into his own hands. He gathered together an offering, and *he* presented it to the Lord. When Samuel arrived, he rebuked Saul, the king of Israel, because he was accountable to Samuel the prophet.

When David scandalized the nation by committing adultery with Bathsheba and by murdering Uriah, Nathan the prophet stood before the king of the nation. He charged him with the crimes because David the king was accountable to Nathan the prophet.

When Nehemiah wanted to travel to Jerusalem and rebuild the city wall, he had to get permission from Artaxerxes because he was accountable to the king for whom he worked as a cupbearer.

When Daniel had to disobey the king and his colleagues, he remained very much at ease. Because he was accountable to God, there was nothing to hide.

One of the things that marked our Lord's life on earth was his submission to the Father's will. The Apostle John tells us on more than one occasion, "Jesus always did the things that pleased the Father."

To the twelve men whom Jesus had selected to be his disciples he passed the torch for the work of the ministry. These men were accountable to him and, ultimately, to each other.

Paul and Silas were accountable to the church at Antioch. Onesimus, the slave, was accountable to Philemon. Timothy was accountable to Paul because the apostle was his father in the faith.

LOVE AND WISDOM

A mentor's "wounds" are those of a faithful friend. Not everyone has the right to climb into your life and offer rebuke. It must be the mentor who has built a love relationship beforehand. Confrontation must be done in a context of love, respect, and trust.

> A mentor's "wounds" are those of a faithful friend. Not everyone has the right to climb into your life and offer rebuke.

A man that I (Ted) mentored, his wife, my wife, Dorothy, and I went out to dinner some years ago. We had very poor service from the waitress, and I chewed her out; I gave her a hard time. As we got out of the restaurant, my friend asked our wives to walk on ahead so he could talk to me. He said, "Ted, you claim that you are a Christian, yet you talked to that girl that way. Now you've lost her respect and mine. You call yourself a Christian leader; you ought to be ashamed of yourself."

He had the liberty to say that to me, and I accepted it. I said, "You're right, I was wrong. I never should have done it, and it was bad on my part." He rebuked me, and this was a man that I was mentoring. You mentor by example, both good and bad.

Confrontation is really the essence of good mentoring. You've got to avoid clichés and address key issues, otherwise time is wasted. Mentoring does not happen in a week or a month. It happens in a period of several months. You have to build trust. You don't confront individuals in the first few meetings. Confrontation is really the hard core of mentoring.

Mentors need wisdom to keep a mentoree accountable in the many and varied problems that are sure to surface. Sometimes an objective opinion will reveal a blind spot in the life of a friend. Sometimes a straight-from-the-shoulder bit of advice will work. Strong reproof will often get a mistaken and/or wayward person back on track. And sometimes a mentor provides a sounding board to listen while a friend puts himself back on target.

Behavior put under close scrutiny tends to change for the better. People who are made accountable to a mentor, a group of friends, a therapy group, a psychiatrist, a pastoral counselor, or a prayer group become serious about changing their behavior.

If God alone is witness, people far too often make all kinds of excuses for their behavior. But if that same person must report to a mentor, he begins to monitor his behavior and improve it.

In times of trouble, a mentor might be called upon merely to listen, to offer a word of advice, and not infrequently to confront the individual with words of rebuke. When there is improvement, invariably it means that the person has been called to account. One word of truth outweighs the world. And one mentor of truth impacts the whole world. That mentor can be you.

### OTHER LEADERS SAY . . .

*"I greatly appreciate the courage it took for Ted Engstrom and Ron Jenson to include this chapter in a book advocating relational mentoring. I say courage because confrontation is a bad word in our North American culture these days, and in many Christian circles it is a 'four-letter*

*word.' In our culture, confrontation equates to intolerance and thus is a deadly sin even if there are no other sins. In the church, we seem to have adopted similar principles and values. In the church we are encouraged to be 'nice' people (defined by me as superficially pleasant at all times so that real relationship is not an option). The Bible implores us to be transparent, loving, gentle, and involved in one another's lives. In short, the Bible teaches us to develop deep, honest friendships—not acquaintanceships, not working relationships, but friendships.*

*"When the authors pointed out that in certain circumstances a mentor must 'invade that person's private world,' they made me cringe. Fear welled up in me at the thought, but this statement reflects biblical principles and values. The Bible insists that we 'go to' those who have something against us. 'Go to' those whom we have something against, and 'go to' those in need of an invasion into their private world. In my experience, church people, including myself, are tremendously reluctant to 'go to' those around us. If we hide in fear from confrontation, then conflicts and sin can persist for generations with no help offered and no resolution achieved."*

—GRAHAM G. BAUGH is a pastor, lawyer, and church consultant living in Langley, British Columbia. He provides consulting services to denominations, churches, and Christian organizations in the areas of conflict resolution, governance, and strategic change.

*"Confrontation is one of the most difficult tasks a mentor must face, and it is simply unwise to try to avoid it. The pivotal moment, and often the toughest one, is initiating the discussion. Here's where preparation can help. Before*

*it is needed, develop a 'contract' with your protégé. My favorite way of initiating such a discussion goes something like this: 'At times, I may need to talk with you about something difficult. My top priority is the long term, so I am willing to go through times that will be tough for both of us. How do you want for me to approach these issues?' While you develop the 'contract' together you are likely to uncover ways to tailor your approach for maximum effectiveness. Be sure to document your 'contract'—including key phrases and decisions—in your notes and perhaps formally with your protégé. When you are faced with a confrontation situation, refer to your notes to season your words and even remind your protégé of the decisions you made together. This type of preparation can help both of you get through the tricky first step and move onto the important work that needs to be accomplished."*

—SARA MOULTON REGER joined the Services Research group at the IBM Almaden Research Center in San Jose, California, in 2003 as one of the first subject matter experts brought over from IBM's Business Consulting Services to initiate this new area of study for IBM. She has been a management consultant for over 16 years, specializing in organizational change, culture transformation, governance, and leadership, both at IBM and at other leading consulting firms.

*"Fear is the enemy's 'weapon of choice' when he wants to keep us from confronting each other. And what are we afraid of? Of being told it's 'none of our business'? Of our input being rejected? Of being perceived as self-righteous? When you look back on your experience, how many times have you reacted that way when someone*

*who loves you confronted you for your own good? For me, it's never happened. Instead, I feel more let down that my mentors didn't confront me when they saw indications that I was heading in a wrong direction or 'driving off the straight and narrow' road. Remember the truth from 2 Timothy 1:7, 'For God hath not given us the spirit of fear, but of power, and of love, and of a sound mind.' Scripture doesn't say 'butter sharpens butter'; it says 'iron sharpens iron.' Pray—ask God for power, love, and a sound mind—and then act."*

—REGI CAMPBELL is a businessman, entrepreneur, and
the author of *About My Father's Business:
Taking Your Faith to Work.*

*"Engstrom and Jensen nail this. Without a willingness to confront in total, but loving, honesty, we cannot expect the disciple-making process to get too far. I love the emphasis on propriety and process. That is, confrontation must be done properly, and it can't be done properly unless it's understood as a process.*

*"Process is going to involve conversation. In his book,* Conversation *(New York: Hidden Spring Books, 2000), Theodore Zeldin, argues that good conversation is critical in any confrontational encounters. 'Real conversation catches fire,' he says and changes people. It's not about merely sending or receiving information; it's about being willing to be changed.*

*"Unfortunately, we live in a MYOB culture, and while minding your own business can often be prudent, in the church, unlike the world, we're called not to mind our own business, but to mind the business of others.*

*"This is not easy, especially since we tend to value love and living in peace with each other over living in healthy relationships with each other and with God. So if, in our mentoring and disciple-making, it appears we may need to confront, we have to realize that our actions may not be perceived as loving, but hostile.*

*"That's why Zeldin promotes healthy conversation, because out of such interaction, new realities emerge. 'Conversation doesn't just reshuffle the cards,' he concludes: 'It creates new cards.'*

*"We call that spiritual maturity, moving closer to the image and likeness of Jesus Christ."*

—TIMOTHY MERRILL is the executive editor of *Homiletics*, a preaching resource for pastors (www.HomileticsOnline.com). He has been a clergyman for a number of years and is the author of *Learning to Fall: A Guide for the Spiritual Clumsy* as well as other books, and articles for the academic press. His "Back Page" column is a favorite among *Homiletics* readers.

*"Confrontation and accountability are two of the most difficult and misunderstood concepts in the Christian walk. We can all think of examples where confrontation was done in an abusive manner, or when sin was ignored because of a fear of confrontation. Both of these extremes are obviously wrong. However, caring confrontation must be understood as foundational for genuine, authentic relationships. One of the distinctives of our lives as Christians should be our willingness to confront others in love and at the same time to be confronted in love. This is what makes us a fully functional 'family' growing together, be-*

*ing built up, becoming mature, and attaining to the whole measure of the fullness of Christ (Ephesians 4:13). Caring enough to confront or be confronted is what allows us to grow. It starts with a genuine willingness to be open to God, his Word, and the exhortation of the Holy Spirit. But it logically extends itself to being truly accountable to one another in the Body of Christ. This allows us to be truly 'one' and demonstrate our unity and real commitment to one another."*

—DR. HENRY KLOPP is a church consultant and is president of the International Graduate School of Ministry, which trains and equips pastors and church leaders worldwide.

## HOW ABOUT YOU?

Determine your level of proficiency in the area of confrontation from the chart below. 1 is the lowest, 10 is the highest with 5 as average.

## CONFRONTATION

| 1 | 1.5 | 2 | 2.5 | 3 | 3.5 | 4 | 4.5 | 5 | 5.5 | 6 | 6.5 | 7 | 7.5 | 8 | 8.5 | 9 | 9.5 | 10 |
|---|-----|---|-----|---|-----|---|-----|---|-----|---|-----|---|-----|---|-----|---|-----|----|

What do you need to do in order to improve half of a point this week in your mentoring relationships?

*"Everyone comes between men's souls and God, either as a brick wall or as a bridge. Either you are leading men to God or you are driving them away."*

—CANON LINDSAY DEWAR

*"If Christ lives in us, controlling our personalities, we will leave glorious marks on the lives we touch. Not because of our lovely characters, but because of his."*

—EUGENIA PRICE

# Chapter 10

# NOW WHAT?

**W**e've covered the nine characteristics of a successful Christian mentor. Encouragement, self-discipline, gentleness, affection, good communication, honesty, servanthood, godliness, and loving confrontation build the foundation for a strong mentoring relationship. Now that you know how a successful mentor thinks, speaks, and acts, you can explore the mentoring possibilities in your life.

Now what? We must respond with personal change in the nine key areas of mentoring. Next, you must commit to the mentoring process and seek to become a mentor and a mentoree. God wants to touch the lives of those around you. The surest way to leave a lasting legacy—regardless of the other aspects of your life—is to mentor people who will commit to mentoring others.

> The surest **way** to leave a lasting **legacy**—regardless of the other **aspects** of your life—is to **mentor** people who will commit to **mentoring others**.

## BE MENTORED

Don't forget that the best mentor also has a mentor. Are *you* accountable to someone outside your family? To someone who can ask hard questions and expect honest answers? Is there someone who is consistently taking a critical look at your life? No one is too advanced to gain from a wise mentorship. Pray for God to give you someone who will encourage you and help you to grow. Many mentoring relationships are begun by the mentoree asking someone older and wiser to mentor her. It doesn't hurt to step out and ask!

Every mentor should also have a mentor. To get the most out of your mentoring experience, do the following:

1. Seek someone who can help you ask the right questions, search in the right places, and stay interested in the right answers.

2. Decide what degree of excellence or perfection you want. Generally the object of mentoring is improvement, not perfection. Perhaps only a few can be truly excellent—but all can be better.

3. Accept a subordinate, learning position. Don't let ego get in the way of learning or trying to impress the mentor with your knowledge or ability and thus set up a mental barrier against learning.

4. Look for a mentor that you respect—but don't idolize him. Respect allows us to accept what he or she is teaching.

5. Put into effect immediately what you are learning.

6. Arrange for an ample and consistent time schedule, select the subject matter in advance, and do your homework to make the sessions profitable.

7. Reward your mentor with your own progress. If you show appreciation but make no progress, the mentor knows he's failed. Your progress is his highest reward.

8. Learn to ask crucial questions—questions that prove you have been thinking between sessions, questions that show progress in your perception.

9. Don't threaten to give up. Let your mentor know that you have made a decision for progress, that he is dealing with a persistent person—a determined winner. Then he knows he is not wasting his time.

We cannot hide if we are to be helped. Committing to a mentoring relationship will give you the skills and arena for personal growth and development. The nine characteristics we've discussed are applicable for both mentors' success and mentorees' development.

Proverbs says, "Pride only breeds quarrels, but wisdom is found in those who take advice" (13:10), "The teaching of the wise is a fountain of life, turning a man from the snares of death" (13:14), "He who ignores discipline comes to poverty and shame, but whoever heeds correction is honored" (13:18), "He who walks with the wise grows wise, but a companion of fools suffers harm" (13:20), "He who listens to a life-giving rebuke will be at home among the wise" (15:31). Take your role as a mentoree as seriously as you take your mentor role, and the Bible says you will grow wise.

## STEPS TO EFFECTIVE MENTORING

A mentor who has the ability to impact the whole world is one who has commitment to go the distance and make a difference in the lives of others. This person gives priority to the kingdom of God and to his righteousness. The process of mentoring is: telling how (education); showing how (demonstration); getting your protégé started (delegation); and keeping them going (evaluation).

How do you choose the right person to mentor? Make a short list of people that you believe in and would like to see grow (whether personally or professionally). Take time to pray for all of the people on your list. Show love and care to all of them as well. But choose to mentor only those that are spiritually responsive and show a strong desire to learn.

Refer to the following guidelines when selecting prospective mentorees:

1. Select a mentoree whose philosophy of life you share.

2. Choose a person with potential whom you genuinely believe in. The secret of mentoring in any field is to help a person get to where he or she is willing to go.

3. Evaluate a mentoree's progress constantly. An honest mentor will be objective. If necessary, he will encourage the person to stay on course, to seek another direction, or even to enter into a relationship with another mentor.

4. Be committed, serious, and available to your mentoree.

### BEGINNING THE MENTORING PROCESS

The following six steps will guide you as you begin the mentoring process:

1. Put into practice the character traits outlined in the previous nine chapters.

2. Find one or more people to encourage you and sharpen you on to growth in the areas that are most difficult for you.

3. Seek out at least one mentoree who can benefit from your life experience, knowledge, and concentrated energy and care.

> Seek out at least one mentoree who can benefit from your life experience, knowledge and concentrated energy and care.

4. Make a commitment to that person. Set specifics such as "We'll meet every other Monday evening from 7:00 to 8:30 p.m. until Christmas."

5. After the specified amount of time has passed, choose to either continue with the current mentoree or select another person to mentor.

6. Keep repeating this process!

Imagine how many lives you can touch! If you mentored just one person each year for the rest of your life, you could possibly impact several dozen individuals. This by itself would be a noteworthy accomplishment. But if each of your mentorees commits to the same process of mentoring (or even if they only mentored a handful of people throughout their lifetime), your faithful example will continue to live on in the lives of hundreds, maybe even thousands, of people.

Consider that you may be an indirect mentor to people *without being aware of it.* No doubt, there are many eyes on you as you make crucial decisions at work. No doubt your children record your every move in their impressionable minds. No doubt that those around you constantly watch to see if you are a person worth following. Therefore, it is imperative that your private life be above reproach.

Your **best** modeling may be letting people **see** how you **handle** your failures and **sinfulness.**

In a similar way, your best modeling may be letting people see how you handle your failures and sinfulness. Jay Bakker says, "The more we encourage people to have a personal relationship with Jesus and the more transparent we can become with one another about our failures, faults, and struggles, the stronger the Church will become."

Every person can benefit from implementing the character traits found in this book. Even if you don't become an "official" mentor, you—and the people around you—will benefit from your exemplary character.

God wants to use *you* to touch the lives of those around you—your family, your friends, the people in your church, the people you work with, and those in your community. If you can embrace this fact that God wants to use you, then you will be all the more motivated to keep your promises and commitments.

Debi Strangland says, "while we are each called to different life experiences, personal interactions, and uses of our gifts and talents, we should always be mindful of how our lives are leading others to a personal relationship with Jesus Christ. Are we building bridges or brick walls?" What will you do with what you've just read? Will you become a legacy builder? The choice is yours.

THE TIME IS SHORT

As a youth, Bill Cosby assumed old people were to look at. "Now," he says, "I am one!" Billy Graham, in his absorbing autobiography, *Just as I Am*, written at age seventy-eight, commented on his surprise at turning old so soon. Ray Ortlund puts the brevity of life in perspective:

"Redeem your time. Buy up every opportunity for living your life right! You say you have seventy years to get it all done. No, you really don't. What did you know about life up to age five? Not much. That leaves sixty-five years. But you sleep twenty-five years or so; so you have only forty years.

"Some years are spent in rest and recreation; some years may be wasted in wickedness or just laziness. How much is left? Not much! And how much total time will you have for your life, anyway? Keats died at twenty-six. Shelly at thirty. Schubert at thirty-one. Alexander the Great at thirty-three. Mozart at thirty-five.

"On the other hand, it's never too late to start really living! Michelangelo began building St. Peter's Cathedral at seventy-six. Verdi was nearly seventy when he composed his "Te Deum." Grandma Moses started painting when she was seventy-eight. Tennyson was writing his greatest lines at eighty-three."

The Scriptures also remind us of life's brevity, "My days are swifter than a runner; they fly away without a glimpse of joy. They skim past like boats of papyrus, like eagles swooping down on their prey" (Job 9:25–26). "The span of my years is as nothing before you. Each man's life is but a breath" (Psalm 39:5). "All men are like grass, and all their glory is like the flowers of the field; the grass withers and the flowers fall, but the word of the Lord stands forever" (1 Peter 1:24–25).

## Get involved. Be willing to step out and try.

As we wrap up the book, our encouragement to you is to get involved. Don't wait until someone asks you; don't wait until you have the time to care; don't wait until you're trained. Get involved. Be willing to step out and try. None of us will have a worldwide impact, but all of us can be changed by those around us. The principles God set down in Scripture are not characteristics that only apostles can emulate. They are ours to put on and ours to give away.

What will you have to show for your life? *Who* will you have to show for your life? It's up to you. Go for it!

## OTHER LEADERS SAY . . .

*"Over the years I have been a mentor to many, and have been mentored by a few; however, I wish I had read this chapter many years ago, as I would have been so much more effective in my mentoring, and would have taken more care to be mentored as well.*

*"Having a chart, a compass, a GPS, and radar equipment to help navigate the stormy and sometimes foggy world we live in is more important than ever before. Our mentors are those navigational helps. Years ago when the world was simpler we looked at the stars with a sextant and navigated the world, but just as those methods are no longer adequate, neither is an ultra simplistic perspective on making our way in this complex and often confusing modern-day world. We need all the help we can get.*

*"Thanks to this chapter we now know what to do next after learning so much about how to live our lives under the guidance and umbrella of the Holy Spirit, along with the guidance of others who are also led by him."*

    —JIM JANZ is a successful Canadian entrepreneur who serves on the board of directors of several Christian ministries. He loves to share the redemption story with all who will listen.

*"From personal experience I can say that mentoring is a powerful tool in achieving real personal growth. A friend*

*of mine says that none of us can see our forehead, and we therefore need to help each see that which we cannot see. We all have these invisible spots of blindness whether it be because of our fallen nature, the cares of the world, or our lack of skills. Mentoring is a process to help us in the areas of our blindness.*

*"To me a mentor can help us to walk in the light as we are commanded to do. In that regard, I think of 1 John 7, 'But if we walk in the light, as he is in the light, we have fellowship with one another, and the blood of Jesus, his Son, purifies us from all sin.'"*

—DENNIS METZLER practiced law in Los Angeles for twelve years. He has also been in several agribusiness, real estate, and investment activities. His principal business activity today is as an investor/developer of commercial real estate in several states. He is on the board of directors at Fuller Seminary and with the Fellowship of Christian Athletes regional board.

*"In November 1991, in a wild leap of faith on my part, I wrote and asked if Ted would consider mentoring me. He graciously consented. And while we often talked about company matters, his greater concern and intent seemed to be in building me.*

*"Ted showed me the biblical basis for mentoring and how it flowed from Barnabas to Paul to Timothy. He suggested that I mentor a younger man.*

*"During the early days of our mentoring relationship a younger man from church asked to spend some time with me on a semi-regular basis. We did and at my suggestion*

*made learning about prayer our focus. Even as we began, he was struggling with progressing multiple sclerosis. He has now gone home to be with our Lord. Our times together were precious to me.*

*"In summary, the years Ted invested in mentoring me have not made me into a little Ted, though I secretly harbored such a desire, and some of him has indeed worn off onto me. Instead, those years of mentoring made an improved Hayne, as he intended."*

—HAYNE BAUCOM has worked with such organizations as Triversal Industries, World Vision, and Atomics International. He was a nuclear engineer, turned computer programmer, turned entrepreneur. He has served multiple ministries through the Christian Management Association and has worked as a counselor and mentor to emerging leaders and new businesses.

*"Ron taught the high school Sunday school class. He loved the young men in his class, and it was obvious to his students. Dan felt the life-long impact of Ron's consistent life in one simple act. Dan had just received his driver's license. After class one Sunday, Ron noticed Dan admiring the 1963 GTO that Ron had just refurbished. Ron tossed the keys to Dan and asked if he would like to 'give it a spin.' That simple act communicated a message of trust and value that further confirmed the words Ron gave each week in class. Today Dan would say he cannot quote any of Ron's Sunday school lessons. But Dan's strong desire to be like Ron eventually led Dan into a full-time pastoral role. Throughout Dan's thirty years in ministry he would admit to giving many young men an invitation to 'give it a spin' accompanied by words of*

*trust. Ron's name is the first one Dan would recall as the person having the most influence in his life."*

—BEV HISLOP is the assistant professor of Pastoral Care to women at Western Seminary in Portland, Oregon.

# INSIGHTS FOR MARKETPLACE MENTORING

O ur goal is to communicate the principles of mentoring to those who desire to leave a legacy of positive change in the lives of those they touch. Yet we also realize that not all mentoring is equal.

There are significant differences between mentoring a brother or sister in the Lord and mentoring in a professional context. Christian to Christian life-mentoring is often holistic and has a strong emphasis on the spiritual dimension. Marketplace mentoring is often business related and emphasizes advancement and accomplishment.

Marketplace mentoring can be just as impacting and rewarding. Below we highlight the particularities of professional mentoring as it relates to the nine characteristics of successful mentors.

**Encouragement:** Every person thrives when they are believed in! Your encouraging words should not be reserved for only those who believe the same as you do. In the corporate world, encouragement can help your protégé take risks, make smart choices, and do what is right.

**Self-Discipline:** Your self-discipline will be a motivation for your protégé to develop personal self-control. Those who cannot control and discipline their thoughts, money, time, possessions, talents, and opportunities will waste their resources. Help your mentoree to gain self-discipline, especially over the areas of life that will affect his success and stability in the future.

**Gentleness:** A gentle spirit communicates deep care for your protégé. Show her that you desire only the best for her life and career by your gentle words and actions. Gentle dealings with your protégé may even make her wonder why you are the way you are. If the question of faith comes up, be honest yet gentle. The apostle Peter said, "Always be prepared to give an answer to everyone who asks you to give the reason for the hope that you have. But do this with gentleness and respect" (1 Peter 3:15).

**Affection:** Jesus illustrated the command to "Love your neighbor as yourself" with a story about a good Samaritan. Though the Samaritan held different beliefs than the Jew he helped, he showed deep love for his "neighbor." Our love for our non-Christian mentorees cannot be different from the love we show to our brothers and sisters in Christ. Your love and concern for your mentoree will show the condition of your heart and will prove your allegiance to God's ways. Show your affection through motivating notes, encouraging phone calls, and respectful physical affirmation such as handshakes and hugs.

**Communication:** Communication with your mentoree must be clear and kind, no matter what or who they believe in. One specific area to be cautious in is that of communicating what you believe. In appropriate situations, you may want to share what you believe or how you have achieved life change through Christ. In these circumstances, it is vital that you communicate accurately and respectfully. Be aware of whether your protégé is really ready to listen to what you have to say and proceed accordingly.

**Honesty:** Honesty cannot be compromised when you are a living example of Christ to your protégé. Since he may hold different values from you, be sure to encourage honesty in every area of life through your words and your actions. If you promote or support dishonest business practices, you will have no room to share the ultimate truth with your mentoree. As a principle, you should seek to be sensitively honest about your life while you encourage them to be honest. Your protégé may seem offensive or misguided in his honesty, but allow him room to share who he really is.

**Servanthood:** Jesus did not reserve his serving for those who believed his message. He gave freely to everyone who asked of him. In the same way, serve your protégé through sacrificing of your comfort level, resources, and time in order to see him grow. We can best lead by serving. As Jesus said, "Whoever wants to be first must be your slave—just as the Son of Man did not come to be served, but to serve, and to give his life as a ransom for many" (Matthew 20:26-28).

**Godliness:** Your godliness can be an example for right living to your protégé—even though she may not know what makes you so different! Godly living is wise and will profit anyone who lives by God's principles whether she believes in him or not. Your godly model will pass along eternal principles for success and happiness in life. For example, the "Golden Rule" applies to the secular arena as well as Christian "circles."

**Confrontation:** As a Christian, you will have to be willing to confront your mentoree if he is involved in illegal or immoral behavior. A mentor has the right to speak into his protégé's life, especially over issues that cannot be compromised. If you need to confront your protégé, refer to chapter nine for hints about confronting in a loving, Christ-like manner.

Many of us spend most of our lives interacting with people without a faith-based commitment. Or there are those whose faith is radically different from the Christian faith, such as Muslims, Hindus, Sikhs, Jewish people, and New Age believers. That is the nature of business. You probably work with multiple people from multiple backgrounds. So, what should you do when you find yourself in this situation?

Can we ignore imparting our life and the life of Jesus Christ into these people (especially if we are managers, owners and/or are spending most of our time with them)? Of course not, we love these people, communicate the love of Christ in appropriate ways, and help people become whole and wise as we model and speak truth around them in positive and practical ways.

Whether your mentoring is in a Christian or professional format, apply the nine characteristics of an effective mentor to see lasting life and vocational change and growth. The results of godly mentoring will outlast your lifetime and reap eternal benefits.

# *About* THE AUTHORS

## TED W. ENGSTROM

As the former president and chief executive officer of World Vision (and now President Emeritus) and a director on numerous boards including Azusa Pacific University and Focus on the Family, Ted W. Engstrom is an influential leader in American religion and social service. He has been the recipient of six honorary doctorates.

Before joining World Vision, Dr. Engstrom was President of Youth for Christ International for six years. He is a management consultant and has conducted the nationwide "Managing your Time" seminars with his colleague Ed Dayton for many years.

An editor and author, Dr. Engstrom has written more than fifty books and hundreds of magazine articles. His books include *The Making of a Christian Leader* (1976), *The Pursuit of Excellence* (Zondervan, 1982), *The Fine Art of Friendship* (Thomas Nelson, 1985), *The Fine Art of Mentoring* (Trinity Press, 1989), *The Effective Board Member* coauthored with Bobb Biehl (Broadman and Holman, 1998) and *Integrity: Character from the Inside Out* coauthored with Robert Larson (Shaw, 2000).

Now in his late eighties, Dr. Engstrom continues to speak, write, and provide leadership training and mentoring.

Dr. Engstrom lives in Bradbury, California. With his late wife, Dorothy, he has three grown children, five grandchildren, and three great grandsons.

# RON JENSON

Ron Jenson is known throughout America and much of the world as America's life-coach, reflecting his expertise in the area of personal leadership development. His doctoral work was in leadership development and included intensive research on the major written works in the field as well as personal interviews with three hundred and fifty of the top leaders in the United States and internationally.

Dr. Ron Jenson is the author of the best-selling book *Achieving Authentic Success* as well as several other books. *Achieving Authentic Success* serves as the foundation of Future Achievement's educational programs, products, and services which are currently sold and distributed in over forty countries through various sales channels including professionals, corporations, non-profit organizations, government sectors, youth, and the family marketplace.

Dr. Jenson is a popular speaker and consultant across a wide variety of venues nationally and internationally.

He has traveled around the world annually for twenty-five years and has spoken to groups including top parliament members in Uganda, twenty thousand business people in India, and corporate and institutional leaders in the U.S. and Europe.

Concerned with the moral and social failings of American and world cultures, Dr. Jenson has turned his attention to the development of programs aimed at rebuilding the mental infrastructure of individuals, families, institutions, and communities. These programs focus on character development and practical life skills and aim at building the tools needed for self-government, which is the key to good family, business, and civil government. Dr. Jenson has worked with presidents of countries and their cabinets to help them achieve their leadership objectives.

Ron Jenson and his team at Future Achievement International specialize in equipping believers to communicate principles from the book of Proverbs to believers and unbelievers alike in appropriate language in a life-coaching context. For more information, check out www.futureachievement.org.

Dr. Jenson has written several books, including *Make a Life, Not Just a Living* (Broadman and Holman, 1998), *How to Succeed the Biblical Way* (Tyndale, 1981), *Life Maximizers* (Honor Books, 1997), and *Fathers and Sons: 10 Life Principles to Make Your Relationship Stronger* coauthored with his son, Matt Jenson (Broadman and Holman, 1998).

Ron and his wife, Mary, live in San Diego. They have two adult children, Matt and Molly.

# Appendix 1
# SUMMARY OF KEY PRINCIPLES

Below is a summary of the key points from each chapter in list form. You can use this tool to review principles or to highlight your personal strengths (add a check mark ✓) and weaknesses (add an X).

CHAPTER 1–ENCOURAGEMENT

❑ 1. Mentors have the ability to see positive change in their mentoree.

❑ 2. Believe in your mentoree's potential and abilities.

❑ 3. Dream of your mentoree's future.

❑ 4. Search for areas of your mentoree's life that are worthy of praise.

❑ 5. Give your mentoree permission to believe in himself.

❑ 6. Don't discourage your mentoree by your silence.

❑ 7. Compliment your mentoree, don't flatter her.

❑ 8. Show your confidence even when your mentoree has made a mistake.

☐ 9. Verbalize your belief in the people you mentor.

☐ 10. Comfort your mentoree with the comfort you have received from God.

☐ 11. Empathize with your mentoree by putting yourself in his shoes.

☐ 12. Choose words that will encourage your mentoree to become the woman or man that God designed them to be.

## CHAPTER 2—SELF-DISCIPLINE

☐ 1. If you don't have self-control, anything can have mastery over you.

☐ 2. Mentors with self-control have learned to set and maintain positive habits.

☐ 3. We cannot tolerate sin in our lives if we hope to be effective.

☐ 4. You can have no say in others' lives when you have no control over your own.

☐ 5. Find an appropriate way to deal with your sins (e.g. confession and repentance).

☐ 6. We can never be too strict with ourselves, if we are pursuing righteousness and a clean conscience before God.

☐ 7. In order to overcome a bad habit, do the following: Discern the problem; discover the biblical alternative; discard the opportunity to sin; disconnect the chain of sin; dwell on your whole relationship with Christ; and drill the new pattern into your life.

❑ 8. You will find victory over sin as you commit to the process of change.

❑ 9. An undisciplined life is often characterized by unwise use of time, money, and other resources.

❑ 10. Consider having a mentor as well as being a mentor.

❑ 11. Even the most seasoned believer has room to grow.

❑ 12. Your personal, growing, living relationship with God is the basis for your mentoring relationships.

❑ 13. The key to God's power to change you is your willingness to concentrate your effort and stick with it until you have formed new habits and have gained self-discipline.

CHAPTER 3—GENTLENESS

❑ 1. Change in your mentoree's life will come through your loving gentleness.

❑ 2. Gentleness is not passive ineffectiveness but tender, caring strength.

❑ 3. Gentleness is not skirting around the issue or giving up before the issue has been addressed.

❑   4. Gentleness is not weakness or ineffectiveness.

❑   5. Gentleness is not a lack of confidence or assertiveness. Rather, gentleness from God gives you a cool-headed ability to assert the truth and confidently stand for what is right.

❑   6. Gentleness is not flattery, nor is it covering over the truth.

❑   7. A gentle person does not shy away from responsibility, including responsibility to speak and act rightly in the life of another.

❑   8. Gentleness is need-oriented and tender.

❑   9. Gentleness is patient.

❑  10. Mentors need to help protégés to discover and practice patterns and methods that work best for them.

❑  11. It is usually best to give *options* in a particular situation, rather than instruct your mentoree on what she *must* do.

❑  12. A mentor keeps his protégé on the right track when making decisions but doesn't demand that things be done the way he wants.

❑  13. Through your gentle strength and sensitive suggestions, your mentoree will have the tools to become more efficient in the workplace, the church, and the home.

❑  14. A gentle attitude may take time to develop.

☐ 1. Affection is practically worked out, but its foundation is in the feelings and convictions of the mentor.

☐ 2. The same care and affection seen in Bible times is greatly needed and equally appropriate today as well.

☐ 3. Focus on your mentoree's strengths in your thoughts of her. Our thoughts dictate our words and our actions.

☐ 4. One of the easiest ways to abort affection for someone is to entertain negative emotions such as anger, un-forgiveness, and bitterness.

☐ 5. Affirmation is the most obvious way to verbally share your affection.

☐ 6. Your protégé expects that the words spoken in your presence will be kept confidential. You can express affection and respect for your mentoree when you honor him by not sharing with others what you know about him.

☐ 7. Ministry flows out of a deep care for those you are ministering to.

☐ 8. While our tendency may be to look at other people's weaknesses, we will never have a deep affection for them until we zero in on their strengths.

☐ 9. Your impact on others has a great deal to do

with a sweet, positive, upbeat attitude and tongue.

❑ 10. Your mouth may be the biggest indicator of your character. It shows where your heart lies and where your priorities are.

❑ 11. Total forgiveness is absolutely essential if we are going to have a positive feeling of committed affection toward other people.

❑ 12. We do not forgive because we are simply trying to be nice, but because we ourselves have already been forgiven by Jesus Christ.

❑ 13. We draw our strength to forgive completely and totally from our heavenly Father who forgave us of wrongs that are deeper than any we have received from others.

❑ 14. Though we may not know what to pray for in specific situations in our mentoree's lives, we can be sure that God always desires for his people to exhibit the fruits of a Spirit-filled life.

CHAPTER 5—COMMUNICATION

❑ 1. In mentoring—as in any significant relationship—effective communication is the backbone.

❑ 2. Good communication is when the "picture" of what I am communicating is the same in the mind of the person I am speaking to as it is in my own mind.

❑ 3. In the process of communication, seek first to understand what your protégé is saying.

❑ 4. Good communication does not result in confusion or misunderstandings.

❑ 5. The need to know the person to whom you are communicating is vital if you really want to communicate effectively.

❑ 6. Just as a word improperly said can be destructive, a word fitly spoken can give new delights, make a plain person into a beautiful person, heal bruises, soothe agitated tempers, give hope to despondent souls, and point the way to God.

❑ 7. In order to always speak truthfully: avoid half-truths; distinguish between fact and opinion; be careful about absolute statements; be honest about yourself; and be careful of white lies.

❑ 8. We are not to speak unless it will build up someone or meet a need.

❑ 9. We should speak when we are encouraging or uplifting people; we should never be cruel; and we should always be truthful.

❑ 10. You will never understand the other person's perspective unless you truly listen to him. Without understanding, communication has not taken place.

❑ 11. With practice, you can develop a "talent" for

listening that will serve you well in the mentoring process.

☐ 12. Ask God for wisdom to assertively understand and meet needs in your protégé's life.

☐ 13. Respond to questions directly and fully, and ask meaningful questions that show you are listening.

☐ 14. Don't try to dodge disagreement or controversy. Simply handle it appropriately: be respectful, listen to the other person, and, if necessary, agree to disagree.

☐ 15. Mentoring should be an intentional time that is reserved for the specific protégé and nothing else.

☐ 16. Often, you can help people reach a conclusion simply by listening and asking intelligent questions.

☐ 17. Asking questions will encourage your protégé and show her that you are listening.

CHAPTER 6—HONESTY

☐ 1. We do not need to hide the fact that we are not perfect. As we gain the ability to be honest before people, we are on the way toward healthy openness and growth.

☐ 2. Honesty involves realizing that you are not perfect and learning how to share your feelings constructively.

☐ 3. God wants us, and waits for us, to ask him to point out areas in our lives that need to be brought into conformity to his will.

☐ 4. Transparency is not an excuse to share all your emotional problems or to live with your emotions on your sleeve.

☐ 5. We are not to think that openness or vulnerability means sharing negative thoughts and feelings in the name of honesty.

☐ 6. Healthy honesty allows others to see weaknesses but does not revel in them.

☐ 7. With the acknowledgment that you are not perfect, you can start to deal with the normal fear of being open.

☐ 8. Mentors do not have to pretend to be perfect; they will be most effective when they can share their own struggles, history, and mistakes. Allow your protégé to watch the process of Christ perfecting you in him.

☐ 9. Your acknowledgment and treatment of sin will shape your mentoree's view and handling of it.

☐ 10. There is no more powerful way to be honest with your mentoree than to let him into your life in a literal sense.

☐ 11. Listening to your mentoree's feelings and emotions involves seeking to understand her.

☐ 12. Avoid statements beginning with "you." These

statements usually come across as a personal attack.

❑ 13. There is much to be said for a strong word that is spoken in love.

❑ 14. Honesty requires sensitivity to timing, character, and level of relationship.

❑ 15. On the human level, complete honesty is appropriate in selected relationships and with particular people.

❑ 16. Unnecessary honesty (that which is reserved for your relationships with God and your most intimate friends) puts a burden on you and your mentoree that will strain the mentoring process.

CHAPTER 7—SERVANTHOOD

❑ 1. If the Master considered foot washing—generally a servant's task—to be his rightful task, perhaps we should take a look at his call for us to serve as he did.

❑ 2. Humility does not imply that we are to have an inferior view of ourselves, but a healthy one.

❑ 3. You cannot underestimate your abilities, background, contacts, position, or any other asset no matter how trivial they may seem. Since they are given by God, they must be handled with great respect and admiration.

❑ 4. Understanding that we are sinful does not mean we need to hate ourselves.

☐ 5. Humility means staying broken and yielded to God on the one hand and resting in the power of God to work through us on the other hand.

☐ 6. If you can maintain brokenness by God's grace, then you will have the foundation of usability before God in your mentoring endeavors.

☐ 7. A truly humble person is one who knows his strengths and his weaknesses, who appreciates both and who learns how to handle both.

☐ 8. A true Christian does not shy away from the work of giving himself to other people, including his mentoree.

☐ 9. But, true servanthood needs no recognition. In fact, it seeks not to be recognized by anyone but God who really is checking our heart and inner motives.

☐ 10. Mentoring is not simply the imparting of new skills or a program by which to lead life. Rather, it is the imparting of character and wisdom that the mentor has gained through experience.

☐ 11. Lead by serving; receive by giving; change lives through love and sacrifice. These values fueled Jesus' highly successful mentoring.

CHAPTER 8—GODLINESS

☐ 1. When God's people are seeking to be like him, he supports that desire by producing godliness in their lives.

❏ 2. Godliness is being like God in thought and behavior. It is a way of living and a way of viewing the world and other people.

❏ 3. The pursuit of holiness in every area of your life will help you to become more godly.

❏ 4. While physical training only lasts as long as the body is well and able, godliness training will last for eternity.

❏ 5. Integrity and consistency in holy living, seriousness about the things of God, correct speech and teaching: these things cannot be looked down on.

❏ 6. Your character can literally shape your mentoree's own character. If you are godly, your mentoree will probably be godly too.

❏ 7. You are a witness and a model; your protégés will watch you as an example of what they should be.

❏ 8. A life patterned after Christ's is godly in the fullest sense. Without being prideful, we can boast of what God has done in our hearts and lives.

❏ 9. If your goal in mentoring is to see your protégé become just like you, then you have a skewed aim. Instead, your goal should be to see your mentoree reach her full potential and become Christ-like.

❏ 10. A godly mentor is above reproach and has a pattern of holiness set deep in his life.

☐ 11. The overarching qualities of a godly mentor are teachability and a willingness to let the Holy Spirit change you.

☐ 12. Godly living reaps the fruit of love, joy, peace, patience, kindness, goodness, faithfulness, gentleness, and self-control in your own life and in your protégé's life!

## CHAPTER 9—CONFRONTATION

☐ 1. Confrontation has a vital part to play in the mentoring relationship: it allows healing, restoration, growth, and, ultimately, victory.

☐ 2. Good mentors love their protégés assertively and patiently shape, challenge, and encourage them.

☐ 3. A mentor who is willing to lovingly confront sin must take measures to safeguard herself and the relationship.

☐ 4. Confrontation can only be successfully done in a context of deep care and respect.

☐ 5. Confronting a mentoree with his wrong should only be done in a safe environment in which both people feel comfortable.

☐ 6. It is essential that confrontation only takes place after much prayer and careful thinking—it cannot be treated lightly or it will have a negative impact.

☐ 7. If possible, limit your confrontation to the main issue and do not bring up lesser, side problems.

❑  8. Regardless of your protégé's response, you should confront with love and prayer.

❑  9. The Scriptures are clear—a healthy mentoring relationship involves a willingness to caringly confront when necessary.

❑  10. You must realize that it is only by the grace of God that you make any progress; and you are to extend the same grace in being long-suffering toward those around you.

❑  11. Maturity is the ability to know how to consistently use the right method at the right time with the right person.

❑  12. God never intends us to look at someone and to make a negative judgment about his or her life.

❑  13. The Bible says that we are to be prayerful, personal, positive, and practical in confrontation.

❑  14. Lives are dramatically changed when people care enough to point out weaknesses in others' lives *for their benefit.*

CHAPTER 10—NOW WHAT?

❑  1. The surest way to leave a lasting legacy— regardless of the other aspects of your life—is to mentor people who will commit to mentoring others.

❑  2. The best mentor also has a mentor.

☐   3. No one is too advanced to gain from a wise mentorship.

☐   4. We cannot hide if we are to be helped.

☐   5. Take your role as a mentoree as seriously as you take your mentor role, and the Bible says you will grow wise.

☐   6. A mentor who has the ability to impact the whole world is one who has commitment to go the distance and make a difference in the life of others.

☐   7. The process of mentoring is: telling how (education); showing how (demonstration); getting your protégé started (delegation); and keeping him going (evaluation).

☐   8. Seek out at least one mentoree who can benefit from your life experience, knowledge, and concentrated energy and care.

☐   9. You may be an indirect mentor to people without being aware of it.

☐  10. Your best modeling may be letting people see how you handle your failures and sinfulness.

☐  11. Even if you don't become an "official" mentor, you—and the people around you—will benefit from your exemplary character.

☐  12. If you can embrace this fact that God wants to use you, then you will be all the more motivated to keep your promises and commitments.

❑ 13. None of us will have a worldwide impact, but all of us can be changed by those around us.

# MENTORING CHARTS

The following charts show some of the men who mentored Ted Engstrom and Ron Jenson and a few of the men and women whom they later mentored. We include these in order to illustrate the multiplication model of mentoring from 2 Timothy 2:2. In this verse, Paul tells Timothy that "the things you have heard me say in the presence of many witnesses [you are to] entrust to reliable men who will also be qualified to teach others."

# MEN WHO MENTORED TED ENGSTROM

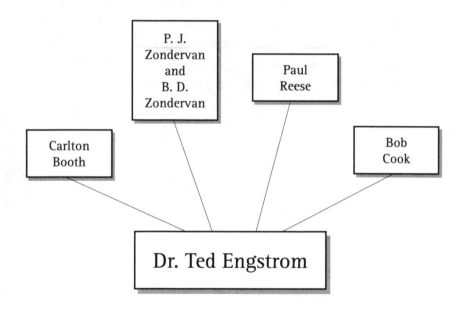

P. J. Zondervan and B. D. Zondervan

Paul Reese

Carlton Booth

Bob Cook

Dr. Ted Engstrom

# TED ENGSTOM'S MENTOREES

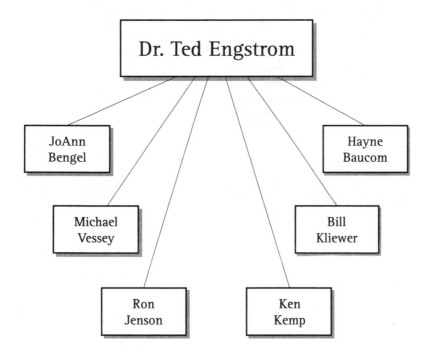

# MEN WHO MENTORED RON JENSON

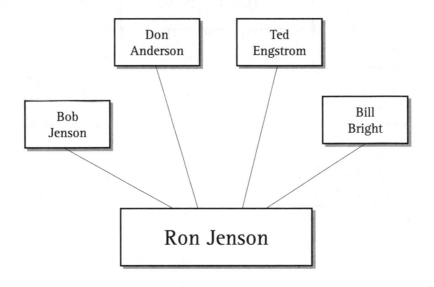

# RON JENSON'S MENTOREES

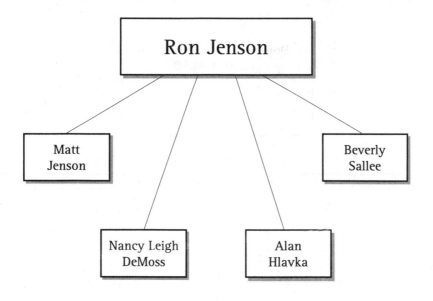

Ron Jenson

Matt Jenson

Beverly Sallee

Nancy Leigh DeMoss

Alan Hlavka

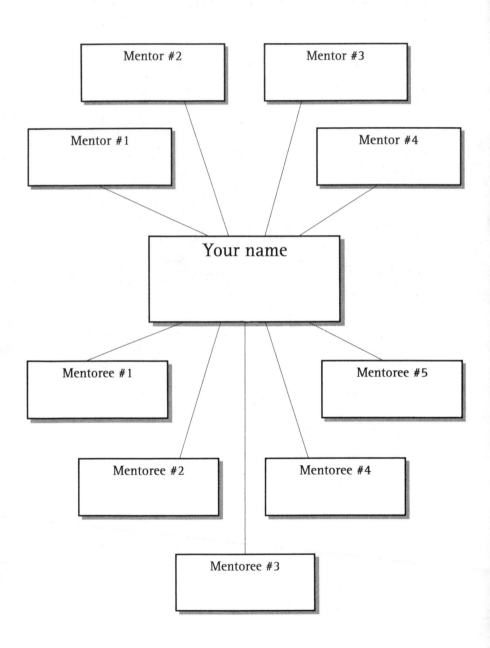

# PERSONAL
## MENTORING CHART

Use the chart on the opposite page to fill in the names of your personal mentors and mentorees. Take the time to dream of the people you would like to have as mentors. Ask God to bring men and women that you can mentor as well.

Think through the individuals who have had or currently have a large impact on your life. Write their names at the top of the chart.

In the bottom section, list the names of those who you have mentored or are currently mentoring.

Consider who could benefit from your time and attention in a mentoring relationship. Write their names on the list below.

INDIVIDUALS I DESIRE TO MENTOR
1.
2.
3.
4.
5.

Dear Reader,

World Vision invites you to share your response to the message of this book by writing to World Vision Press at worldvisionpress@worldvision.org or by calling 800-777-7752.

For information about other World Vision Press publications, visit us at www.worldvision.org/worldvisionpress.